THE AUTHOR

Earl R. Wasserman holds the Ph.D. degree in English from The Johns Hopkins University and for ten years was a member of the English department of the University of Illinois. In 1948 he returned to Johns Hopkins as Associate Professor of English. An editor of *E L H, A Journal of Literary History* and *Modern Language Notes*, he is also the author of *Elizabethan Poetry in the Eighteenth Century* and is presently at work on a study of the poetry of Shelley.

The Finer Tone

KEATS' MAJOR POEMS

The Finer Tone

KEATS' MAJOR POEMS

> . . . *another favorite Speculation of mine,*
> *that we shall enjoy ourselves here after*
> *by having what we called happiness on*
> *Earth repeated in a finer tone and so*
> *repeated.*
> — Keats to Benjamin Bailey,
> November 22, 1817

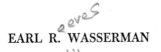

EARL R. WASSERMAN

1953

THE JOHNS HOPKINS PRESS BALTIMORE

To the memory of

LINDA SUZANNE WASSERMAN

Table of Contents

The Finer Tone

KEATS' MAJOR POEMS

Foreword

$\mathcal{T}$HE READINGS of Keats' poems that make up this book are based on a few critical premises that seem to be growing heretical. The central premise is that poetry communicates not only by the means available to all verbal expressions but also by those that are the special and exclusive property of poetry. The assumption is simple and obvious enough—or it would be if it were not for a new innocence in criticism that dwells on the second half of this premise and minimizes the first. The new critic insists that a poem be examined as a poem and not as another thing, but he has constricted this excellent principle until it has very nearly come to mean that everything communicated by the poem is defined within its own boundaries and nowhere else. I state this constriction in extreme form because, although most explicators are sensible men and know the need of reaching outside the text for information, it is clear that they resent the act, engage in a ritual of verbal self-flagellation for occasional transgressions, and wish the work of art were so self-sufficient it could not tempt them to sin.

It is easy to understand how this anti-intellectualism has come about, for a kind of pedantry, operating as though art were affirmation, had been extracting from poetry a philosophy, a theology, an ethics, a biography, and had neglected its peculiar mode of existence as poetry in favor of its existence as only another thing. The same pedantry had also been inclined to impose upon a poem an order of things that, " research " had indicated, may have been relevant in some way to the artist, but that is not necessarily consonant with what the internal workings of the poem are saying. In its corrective extravagance, however, the new innocence has gone to the opposite extreme and, too jealously guarding the

[3]

integrity of poetry, has made many critics neurotically fearful of using means outside the poem to explicate it. The scholar who can supply extra-textual information has consequently become a kind of rich uncle who, having made a fortune in sewage, is handy to have around for assistance but is not introduced to the guests.

Before it is anything else, a poem is an expression in the form of words, and words do not contain their own meaning. Their extra-textual meaning is the result of a convention that is recorded, insofar as possible, in dictionaries and encyclopedias—sources as much outside the poem as the convention is. This is a trivial point to make, for I am certain no sane explicator will deny it; but it may be extended in a direction that some have not been inclined to admit. Words may also have special private meanings, values that the poet attaches to them in order to make the frail verbal forms carry the full freight of his intention: witness Wordsworth's "power" and "presence," Shelley's "splendor," Keats' "happiness," Yeats' "gyres." The special value of these words may be only presupposed in a given poem, and only an examination of the word in its various contexts in all the author's works will give insight into that special value. The danger lies only in assuming the special value in a given appearance without observing how the context qualifies it and whether it is necessarily relevant. But if we are fortunate enough to have even a scrap of paper on which the poet has recorded a clue to that private meaning it would be a precious form of intellectual asceticism not to test its relevance; and it would be an equally profitless asceticism to avoid a book on philosophy or a biographical fact if they are pertinent to shaping the significance of the poet's words. For once the defender of critical exclusion consults the *New English Dictionary*, he cannot well question our even more distant excursions from the text. He can only question whether the return trip truly gets us home.

Our corruption, like original sin, may turn out to be a Fortunate Fall.

Most important—and the end towards which I am driving—the theory of critical purity brushes aside the fact that, although a work of art is an organism, it must exist inside some frame of reference, which may not be explicit in it, and yet in whose terms alone it is organic. Beethoven's *Pastoral Symphony* would not be organic with respect to El Greco's *View of Toledo*, and yet both are organisms. Without reference to epic conventions, the contest, the extended similes, and the divine council in Swift's *Battle of the Books* fail to be integral; it is only when we bring to the work the pre-existing and assumed framework of the epic that these matters take on their organic functions. The lyrics in Gay's *Beggar's Opera* have their own charm and bite, but their full force and their interrelation with the other elements of the play derive from their being read against the echoing-wall of the original ballads to whose tunes they are set. No amount of probing within the opera will conjure up the words of these popular ballads, and yet they are as much an operative part of the play and a control over its meaning as if they were printed there. If " scholarship " is the work of making available to us these implicit artistic controls, then " scholarship " is indispensable to an intelligent and full explication.

We cannot, however, limit ourselves to genres, literary allusions, and historical events as patterns that must be brought to certain works of art. Every composition must be created from some perspective, some special ordering of things and experience. Only the Creator, I trust, knows Order itself. The special ordering may not—probably will not—be ours, and it will probably be assimilated into the work of art, rather than explicitly stated in it. If we isolate Wordsworth's " Solitary Reaper " as though it were an anonymous poem, it appears to be ordered only as a casual experience of the poet; under special circumstances he hears a girl sing, is impressed, and carries away the song in his heart. However, in terms of the pantheistic ontology that truly gives the poem its design, the girl's song assumes a symbolic value as "something far more deeply interfused" which allows the "mere fact" of the event to be "exhibited as connected with that infinity without which there is no poetry." In the light of this controlling framework such matters as the poet's retaining the music "Long after it was heard no more" are considerably more functional within the poem than they would be if it were shaped only as a personal event.

The poem, then, cannot be fully defined from the inside alone; it is also defined by the way it performs in a special system of things. Read in a different ontology, the "Solitary Reaper" becomes not only a different poem, but a far less organic one: it becomes Euclidean geometry in a non-Euclidean universe. Yet, knowledge of the relevant system of things can often be gained only by a study of the entire corpus of the author's writings and even by a study of the thought of his contemporaries. (From these premises concerning the existence of a work of art certain implications seem to follow that have to do with the nature of literature at large; but I shall delay these considerations until I have attempted to make practical application of the premises by reading Keats' poems.)

It is with no sense of embarrassment, then, that I have used some of Keats' poems to explain others, have combed his letters and other prose for clues to intentions out of which he formed poems, and have even sought aid from a probable "source" poem. I have read the poems as verbal communications, and therefore have searched for relevant information wherever I could find it. I have done so, not only in order to understand the individual words, but especially to discover the presuppositions within which each poem has its being and from which it derives its complex oneness.

The only justifiable objection to this mode of reading is not that it is wrong, but that it is not enough. If I am insistent upon the interpretive use of what is usually labeled " scholarship," I am equally insistent that critical analysis cause the relevant " scholarship " to converge upon the center of the poem as poem. The final goal of a critical reading is not to discover the universe in which the work functions, but the way it functions in that universe. Poetry is a very special form of verbal communication, and by very special means, such as meter, stanzaic pattern, total structure, the dramatic disposition and movement of the images, a more than usually flexible syntax, and the arousing of affective responses in the reader, it both qualifies the extra-contextual meanings of the words and also makes nonverbal statements. It is in examining the " interinanimation " of all these elements that one is examining poem as poem and not as another thing. Nevertheless, what is being communicated by purely poetic means—indeed, the relevance of what they are communicating—can be determined only after the poem is first exhaustively understood as something more general; that is, as all other verbal communications are understood.

I certainly do not mean, therefore, to separate the following explications wholly from the procedures of those who want to examine poems as art. I hope my ultimate purpose is the same as theirs. Indeed, my main intention in the following chapters is to unfold the richness I believe to be contained within Keats' major poems by probing beyond their verbal level and seeking to learn both how their *poetry* qualifies the surface meaning and what the *poetry*, as distinct from merely verbal content, states in itself. This, I believe, is the kind of reading Keats' poems require but have seldom received because they are not usually assumed to be organisms, but only loosely associated decorative pictures and moods provoked by the poet's longing for luxurious sensuous experiences. Keats is assumed to be a poet who "loved beauty for its own sake" (whatever that may mean), and therefore his works may be intoned, marveled at, and wallowed in like a perfumed bath, but must not be examined analytically. It is one of the paradoxes of literary studies that although the scholar has acquired an impressive body of learning about the Romantic poets, he has seldom brought that learning to bear upon the internality of their art. Curiously, he has learned a prodigious amount about Shelley's readings in Platonism, about Coleridge's theory of the imagination, about Keats' debt to Milton; but when he comes to read their poetry as art he tends to call upon only his affective responses and finds in Keats, for example, only richly decorative effects. He trusts his head to accumulate facts about the poetry, but his feelings to experience the poem; and seldom does he consider the possibility that if he elected a relevant frame of reference he would find Keats using head and heart, and both at the same time.

If the explications that follow have any validity, it appears to me that Keats emerges from them as one of the great masters of what I choose to call autonomous poetry, poetry whose energy lies within the work itself and is generated by the organic interactions of its component members. This is not the only kind of poetry, for we might distinguish it from, let us say, much of Wordsworth's, whose energy often depends to a greater degree upon the reader's psychological relations to it. Granting the contributory part that affective response plays in the total workings of Keats' poems, they are self-contained organisms, each having its own vitality so that the prose element and the purely poetic forces (structure, imagery, meter, etc.) are interdependent in shaping the full import. Affective response is usually only one of these shaping elements. On the other hand, granting that such a poem as the " Solitary Reaper " is also a self-contained organism gaining its vitality from what its elements do to each other inside the poem, Wordsworth's poetry generally ("Lucy Gray," for example) tends to draw its meaning mainly from the evolving effect it has upon the reader's mind and feelings and to become organic essentially as an affective experience. A search for a complexity within the texture of his poems yields rather thin results. Consequently, these two forms of poetry require two different modes of explication. The first must be examined in terms of a living organism, the second in terms of the psychology of an organic experience. I am not, then, advocating that the manner of explication employed here is pertinent to all poetry or that poetry is good or bad in proportion as it yields itself to this method. I use this explicatory manner here because I believe it corresponds to the peculiar mode of poetic existence possessed by *Keats'* poems; and I believe it corresponds to that mode because I believe that mode is consonant with Keats' metaphysics—not Wordsworth's or mine or anyone else's.

* * *

The apparently unusual order of the chapters is the result of expediency. Since the " Ode on a Grecian Urn " can be unfolded with least dependence upon Keats' other poems and embraces almost the entire range of his poetic thought, it has been placed first as a kind of prologue; the order of the other poems has been determined by the degree to which they are helpful in laying the groundwork for further explications.

I have limited myself to five poems because they are the only major poems by Keats that I have learned to read to my own satisfaction. My only regret is that I have not learned to read the " Ode to Psyche," for I believe it is a major poem and is still to be understood. By the definition of my purpose I have excluded the brief lyrics and the sonnets, though the latter are often richly complex. "Isabella" and the other odes I consider lesser poems in that the full statements they have to make lie very near the surface. The two pieces on Hyperion are fragments; they lack a total structure, cannot be organic wholes, and therefore cannot be explicated, in the full sense of that word. Although I believe *Endymion* has a greater over-all design than is usually granted, it is too sprawling to lend itself to close analysis.

Ode on a Grecian Urn

I

Thou still unravish'd bride of quietness,
 Thou foster-child of silence and slow time,
Sylvan historian, who canst thus express
 A flowery tale more sweetly than our rhyme:
5 What leaf-fring'd legend haunts about thy shape   c
   Of deities or mortals, or of both,   d
    In Tempe or the dales of Arcady?   e
  What men or gods are these? What maidens loth?   d
   What mad pursuit? What struggle to escape?   c
10   What pipes and timbrels? What wild ecstasy?   e

II

Heard melodies are sweet, but those unheard
 Are sweeter; therefore, ye soft pipes, play on;
Not to the sensual ear, but, more endear'd,
 Pipe to the spirit ditties of no tone:
15 Fair youth, beneath the trees, thou canst not leave   c
   Thy song, nor ever can those trees be bare;   d
    Bold Lover, never, never canst thou kiss,   e
  Though winning near the goal—yet, do not grieve;   c
   She cannot fade, though thou hast not thy bliss,   e
20   For ever wilt thou love, and she be fair!   d

III

Ah, happy, happy boughs! that cannot shed
 Your leaves, nor ever bid the Spring adieu;
And, happy melodist, unwearied,
 For ever piping songs for ever new;
25 More happy love! more happy, happy love!   c
  For ever warm and still to be enjoy'd,   d
   For ever panting, and for ever young;   e

All breathing human passion far above,   c
  That leaves a heart high-sorrowful and cloy'd,   d
30   A burning forehead, and a parching tongue.   e

IV

Who are these coming to the sacrifice?
  To what green altar, O mysterious priest,
Lead'st thou that heifer lowing at the skies,
  And all her silken flanks with garlands drest?
35 What little town by river or sea shore,   c
  Or mountain-built with peaceful citadel,   d
    Is emptied of this folk, this pious morn?   e
And, little town, thy streets for evermore   c
  Will silent be; and not a soul to tell   d
40   Why thou art desolate, can e'er return.   e

V

O Attic shape! Fair attitude! with brede
  Of marble men and maidens overwrought,
With forest branches and the trodden weed;
  Thou, silent form, dost tease us out of thought
45 As doth eternity: Cold Pastoral!   c
  When old age shall this generation waste,   d
    Thou shalt remain, in midst of other woe   e
Than ours, a friend to man, to whom thou say'st,   d
  Beauty is truth, truth beauty,—that is all   c
50   Ye know on earth, and all ye need to know.   e

Ode on a Grecian Urn

i

BECAUSE THE assertion that beauty is truth has the illusory appearance of being the most explicit and most meaningful statement in the " Ode on a Grecian Urn," nearly all examinations of the poem have concentrated on the concluding lines, only to discover that the apparently clear abstractions are an *ignis fatuus*, beckoning to a morass of quasi-philosophy. What is beguiling about the final aphorism is that the precise instruments with which to probe its grammar and rhetorical emphasis are available to us; and yet they alone have been unable to make it give up a meaning that the total poem justifies. The more inclusive we make the terms "beauty" and "truth," theoretically the more intelligible they become by embracing all special meanings; and the assertion in which they are contained equates them with the syntactical preciseness of a mathematical statement, Keats even interchanging subject and predicate so that the equation may be read in either direction: beauty is truth, truth beauty. Nevertheless, the more we tug at the final lines of the ode, the more the noose of their meaning strangles our comprehension of the poem. Even so acute a reader as T. S. Eliot has written that the aphorism "strikes me as a serious blemish on a beautiful poem; and the reason must be either that I fail to understand it, or that it is a statement which is untrue." The aphorism is all the more beguiling because it appears near the end of the poem, for its apparently climactic position has generally led to the assumption that it is the abstract summation of the poem, detachable from the first forty-eight lines and equal to them.

But the ode is not an abstract statement or an excursion into philosophy. It is a poem about things: an urn, pipes, trees, lovers, a priest, a town; and poetic images have a grammar of their own that is contained in their dramatic actions. For this meta-grammar of poetic imagery, this grammar that transcends verbal grammar, we have no technical terms and hence no formalized methods of analysis; and yet we must read an imagistic poem with the same analytical frame of mind that we adopt towards a prose sentence so as to discover relationships, relative significances, and emphases. We need to ask such questions as: Are " deities " and " mortals " (6) two nouns, as they certainly are in their merely verbal grammar, or do they act out the role of a hyphenated noun in their imagistic grammar? What is the imagistic syntax of pipes, lovers, and trees in stanza two? Does the drama of the last two stanzas enact an independent clause or a dependent clause in the sentence which the entire poem enacts? For only a reading of the total imagistic grammar of the poem can unfold its intent, as the final lines alone cannot. Indeed, through such a total reading, the aphorism proves not to be a summation of the poem, nor even the high point of its intent, but only a subordinate functional part of the grammar of images.

ii

Let us first assume the loosest possible framework for the poem and then observe the way in which the actions of the images qualify and orient the general meaning. No one will deny that the ode, like most of Keats' poems, deals with the human and mutable on the one hand, and the immortal and essential on the other; and that what it states has something to do with both an opposition and a fusion of these two states. On this note the poem opens, for the poet softly addresses the urn as a " still unravish'd bride."

Now, such tender reverence for what normally is an undesirable condition—to say nothing of the startling force of the word " unravish'd " as applied to " bride "—calls for some inquiry. Between the realm of the merely human, where passion leaves " a heart high-sorrowful and cloy'd," and the immortal, where " Real are the dreams of Gods," [1] there is in Keats' cosmology the knife-edge where the two meet and are indistinguishably present. On the shores of darkness, Keats wrote, " there is light, / And precipices show untrodden green; / There is a budding morrow in midnight." [2] To Homer, the prototype of the poet, he added, such imaginative insight was granted that, although physically blind, he could penetrate into the nature of things so as to perceive, beyond their outward forms, the essence of light, which contains both light and darkness, and the essence of day, which contains both midnight and morning. The power that perceives this paradoxical essence is an equally paradoxical " blindness keen."

For the expression of this paradoxical essence I shall borrow Kenneth Burke's excellent term " mystic oxymoron " [3] in order to designate not merely the paradoxical collocation of contraries (e. g., freezing heat) but the mystic interfusion of these contraries. To this point of mystic oxymoron and no farther, Keats held, can the human imagination occasionally and momentarily rise as it seeks to overcome the weariness, the fever, and the fret. In *Endymion*, the worshippers of Pan pray that the earth-god

> *Be still the unimaginable lodge*
> *For solitary thinkings; such as dodge*
> *Conception to the very bourne of heaven,*
> *Then leave the naked brain: be still the leaven,*
> *That spreading in this dull and clodded earth*

---

[1] " Lamia," I. 127.

[2] " To Homer."

[3] Kenneth Burke, *Grammar of Motives* (New York, 1945). I am conscious of having monotonously overused the term, but I know no other way of expressing simply the central principle of Keats' visions.

Gives it a touch ethereal—a new birth:
Be still a symbol of immensity;
A firmament reflected in a sea;
An element filling the space between;
An unknown—but no more.[4]

Were Pan more, he would be an unknowable, outside man's range, beyond the bourne, and therefore in the realm of pure immortality, which, in Keats' theology, can never be the home of man either in this life or in the next. Instead, Pan is the concurrence of the mortal and immortal, and hence a knowable unknown without being any the less unknown: he invests the physical with the ethereal; he is the perceptible reflection of the imperceptible; his is the oxymoronic nature of heaven's bourne.

Although the ode is a symbolic action in terms of an urn, its intrinsic theme is that region where earth and the ethereal, light and darkness, time and no-time become one; and what the symbolic drama ultimately discovers is the way in which art (the urn) relates man to that region. For the bourne of heaven is the outermost limit of the imagination after it has left naked the materialistic brain, which tries to seize everything in a clear, and therefore merely earthly, conception. Moreover, this area where mortal and immortal become one without destroying each other is the goal that almost everywhere conditions Keats' values and poetic perceptions to such a degree that his poetry must be read in the light of the ontology its oxymoronic nature implies.

To this area of mystic oxymoron the unravished bride very nearly belongs. On the literal level, the urn has existed in the physical world, in which all things are mutable, and so is related to aspects of time and sound. And yet, by enduring long, it has not only caused them to become secondary factors in its existence (an unravished *bride*, and a *foster*-child), but has become related to

[4] *Endymion*, I. 293-302.

[16]

their dimensional negatives: quietness, silence, slow time. It exists amid dimensions, and yet, by resisting their usual destructive effects, is tending to make them irrelevant to its existence. In another sense also it approaches the bourne of heaven, for " bride," suggesting the first phase of the process of generation, has reference to the human and mutable, and consequently has the same paradoxical relation to " unravish'd " that morrow has to midnight: the urn belongs to both becoming and immutability, the fluid and the fixed. But the urn only approaches this region, since the statement that it is *still* unravished carries with it the threat that it eventually may be ravished, and since it is related to slow time rather than to no-time. The deceleration is only moving the urn in the direction of the extra-temporal.

This same hesitantly suggested collocation of the mortal and the immortal, and of the dynamic and the static, makes up the loose fabric of the entire first stanza. The figures on the urn are deities or mortals—or both (6) ; and the emphasis lies on the last suggestion, especially as Keats repeats his doubt, interchanging the terms to blur their difference: " What men or gods are these? " (8) Mortal and immortal move close to the knife-edge, but Keats' question, although it brings them together in the same context, expresses a hesitation that prevents them from fusing. The same loose mingling appears in the line " In Tempe or the dales of Arcady " (7), Tempe being that earthly region which the gods, especially Apollo, were inclined to favor—an earthly heaven—and Arcady that region that man thought to approach most nearly a paradise—a heavenly earth. In each name both the divine and the mortal are present, but with inverted emphasis.

Moreover, the urn itself embodies both conditions, but only in its two different roles ; and thus the opposites become associated but still fail to coalesce. As total urn it is related to silence and slow time ; yet the figures on the frieze that the quiet urn contains are characterized by their quick and energetic movements and by their music, made noisy by the explosive-laden words "pipes" and "timbrels." Silence and sound, the timeless and the timeful, are nicely counterpoised by the imagery, the music, and the tempo of the stanza.

Finally, the urn, although a bride, is still unravished; the maidens, although unmarried, are in imminent danger of ravishment. The urn, although it has been for ages in the world of mutable becoming, has been unaffected by the acts that belong to becoming because it is not alive; mortality is not its vital principle. The maidens, although their chastity relates them to the world of pure and changeless being, seem about to be despoiled this very moment by the generative act that symbolizes the world of becoming; because they are mortal, mutability and decay are their vital principle.

But just as the slightest shift of our glance brings to us now the nearly eternal urn, and now the nearly fleeting movements of the pastoral scene on it, so the two qualities, stasis and flux, are not sharply juxtaposed. Each term of the opposition is blunted by containing its own contrary, for Keats is shaping the terms, not to mark the dichotomy, but to nudge them towards a fusion. Hence, all the sense of transient action in the last three lines, since it has been communicated by a motionless marble relief, is properly carried by nouns and adjectives rather than by verbs. The apparently transitory movement does not take place; it is named or described as though it were captured and held rigid. We do not hear the tune, but see the instruments; the men do not pursue, but there is pursuit; the maidens are not struggling, but there is struggle; and the tension between "struggle" and "escape" further moves the activity towards a taut stasis. A slight acceleration of slow time would put the apparently static urn in the flowing current of change; and a slight tug would wholly remove from time the apparently energetic figures of the frieze. Like the humanity and/or divinity of the figures, like the marriage-chastity of the urn and the virginity-ravishment of the maidens, the immortality of the urn and the temporality of the figures are delicately poised on each side of heaven's bourne, yearning towards that area of mystic interfusion to which solitary thinkings can mount " —but no more."

The only linkage between the frieze and the urn is made by the line " What leaf-fring'd legend haunts about thy shape " (5), and the paradoxical vagueness of the words " haunts about " makes that relationship fluid, malleable, instead of fixed. The frieze is not superimposed upon the urn or juxtaposed to it; it is the spectral essence that is independent of the urn and yet, at the same time, is diffused through the urn's atmosphere. This paradox of indwelling and independence is the precondition for oxymoronic fusion. The long period making up the stanza, beginning softly and slowly, and becoming breathlessly excited in the staccato series of questions, finally reaches its climax in the words " wild ecstasy." The ecstasy brings together the pursuit and the music, the human and the superhuman, and, by conveying an impression of exquisite sense-spirit intensity, leads us to that fine edge between mortal and immortal where passion is so intense that it refines itself into the essence of ecstasy, which is without passion. " Ecstasy " is therefore both the end towards which the dramatic action of the symbols has been moving, and also the means of entry into the second stanza.

In the second stanza all the nearly antithetical elements of the first now rush together and coalesce. There is song; and yet it is unheard, is played to the spirit, and has no tone—that is, none of those accidents that impart to the essence of song a distinctive and audible quality, and yet whose removal does not deny the song-ness. When Endymion had entered into a mystical union with spirit so that " His every sense had grown / Ethereal for plea-sure," to him, too, " Silence was music from the holy spheres." [5] The silence of the urn and the sound of the pipes and timbrels have run together. The chastity and marriage of the urn, the pursuit and escape of the human figures, are also resolved in an area where time blends with no-time; where the infinity of " For ever wilt thou love, and she be fair! " (20) is born out of the immediacy of "never canst thou kiss, / Though winning near the goal " (17–18).

The marriage-chastity of the urn and the virginity-ravishment of the maidens now intermingle: the lover can never kiss, though winning near the goal, and yet he will love for ever. Urn and maidens have coalesced in this chaste ravishing, for, by being stretched out into an infinity of time, the passionate pursuit can never be completed to become a destruction. The maidens now partake of the " still unravish'd " condition of the urn, not because, like the urn, they are untouched by the ravishing, but because the pursuit is protracted into infinity. On one side there is loving; on the other, loved. But between lies the vital essence of love, a ravishing that can never become ravishment.

iii

Before we can follow further the dramatic action of the sym-bols, we must return to stanza one to gather up a cluster of images. The urn, we are told, is a " sylvan " historian, its tale " flowery," and its legend " leaf-fring'd." It is both outwardly and inwardly woodland, for the frieze has a border of leaves about it, and the scene depicted within the frieze is sylvan. Second, the men and maidens are in the throes of the love-pursuit. And finally the pipes and timbrels are the symbols of music. In the first stanza these

[5] *Ibid.*, II. 671-75.

images—trees, lovers, and song—hover just below the level of the main sense and appear in almost random positions. " Sylvan," " flowery," and " leaf-fring'd " are adjectival, perceptible only through the translucency of the nouns whose property they are. Only our fecund talent for recognizing the rapacity of love, and not anything in the explicit description, leads us to see the pursuit and struggle as a love-game instead of a brutality; and it is significant that instead of " What mad pursuit? " Keats originally wrote, " What love? what dance," but revised, no doubt in order to keep the image of the lovers beneath the threshold of conscious attention. Finally, the pipes and timbrels are also somewhat slighted as they are shuffled into the rapid succession of love symbols. Through the tissue of the first stanza these three images are only emergent.

In the second stanza the originally subliminal images have become the central theme. The entire stanza works towards fixing the three images in heaven's bourne, where sound is so intense as to be inaudible, the maturation of nature so intense as to be without growth or decay, and the consummating of love so intense as to be without consummation. The images are now on the surface of the poetic texture, the least attention being given to the trees, more to the song, and most to the lovers; but they still tend to be scattered and intermingled, falling into no obvious pattern of relative significances.

To say, however, that the three images have emerged dramatically into a significance is to concentrate on the movement of the images alone. In the more obvious sense, the three images do evolve; in another, Keats and the reader are being drawn empathically into the action in the frieze, although the surface of the poem is wholly a drama of the symbols, and the poet's involvement in the drama appears only in the implications of the imagistic grammar. When the total personified urn is the object of attention at the beginning of stanza one, the three images are presented to a subordinate level of consciousness, just as they are subordinate physically to the real urn itself. But they loom larger in proportion as Keats, appearing only in the mode in which the action is expressed, increasingly enters into a participation in the life of the images. Or, conversely, Keats' empathic participation in the images increases as the images grow larger upon the consciousness.

The key to a reading of the ode, then, is the perception of these triune movements in the first two stanzas: (1) the gradual emergence of the three images, (2) the gradual absorption of the poet into the three images, and (3) the convergence of the immortal-essential and the temporal-physical towards a point of fusion where these categorical distinctions are blotted out. These are not three parallel dramas, but different manifestations of the same one. The converging movements of the transitory and the eternal to the point where songs are refined of tone to become the vital essence of song, and the empathic entrance of the poet into the essence of the scene, for example, exist only in each other.

iv

In order to follow the action of the images into the third stanza, which, largely because of the repetition of the word "happy," has usually been condemned as a sentimental lingering over the scene, it would be helpful to know the significance of this word in Keats' vocabulary. If the word "happy" suggests only sudden girlish rapture, it no doubt is unpleasant, and the stanza a failure. But this is to grant Keats only the lowest level of meaning for the word, whose value has shrunk greatly since Pope concluded his *Essay on Man* with an epistle on the "Nature and State of Man with respect to Happiness" and Dr. Johnson sent Rasselas in search of happiness. The clue to the very special value the word had for Keats lies in a passage in *Endymion* beginning, "Wherein

lies happiness?" [6]—a passage that he singled out as of extraordinary importance in the ways of his poetic mind. When I wrote
it, he declared, " it was a regular stepping of the Imagination
towards a Truth. My having written that Argument will perhaps
be of the greatest Service to me of any thing I ever did. It set
before me at once the gradations of Happiness even like a kind
of Pleasure Thermometer." [7] Keats has cautioned, in effect, that
not only *Endymion* but all his subsequent poetry probably should
be read with reference to this pleasure thermometer—although
one may wish he had chosen a name for it that savors less of
Leigh Hunt and his precious coterie. The argument of the passage
to which Keats refers is that " happiness " lies

> *In that which becks*
> *Our ready minds to fellowship divine,*
> *A fellowship with essence; till we shine,*
> *Full alchemiz'd, and free of space. Behold*
> *The clear religion of heaven!*

Happiness, then, is no cheap gaiety, but the *summum bonum*,
the opposite of the weariness, the fever, and the fret that are the
inherent attributes of the unhappy mortal world. It lies, we notice,
in that which beckons us until we are free of the spatial, that
extension which is the opposite of essence; and freedom from
space begins at heaven's bourne, the point of mystic blending. If
boughs can beckon us there, then happiness lies *in* them, just as
we assume a greenness in leaves if they have within themselves
the property of provoking in us a perception of greenness; and
Keats, in his own vocabulary, has as much justification in calling
the boughs " happy boughs " as we have in calling the leaves
" green leaves." Indeed, to describe the boughs, instead of the self,
as " happy " is linguistically consistent with Keats' premise of

[6] *Ibid.*, I. 777.
[7] Letter to Taylor, January 30, 1818.

empathy, for the happiness resides not in the self, but in the object into which the self is transported and in which it experiences. We also notice that these things of happiness entice

Our ready minds to fellowship divine,
A fellowship with essence

—which is a more poetical way of expressing what I have described as Keats' empathic entrance into the life of the frieze, the vital core of the urn. For lack of another term I am using the word " empathy " here to describe, not the ego's attribution of the modes of its own activity to outward forms, but the act of freeing the self of its identity and its existence in time and space, and consequently the act of mystic absorption into the essence of outward forms. In this latter sense the doctrine of empathy is one of the cardinal principles of Keats' poetic and religious creed. " Men of Genius," he declared, " are great as certain ethereal Chemicals operating on the Mass of neutral intellect—[but] they have not any individuality, any determined Character." [8]

As to the poetical Character itself (I mean that sort of which, if I am any thing, I am a Member; that sort distinguished from the wordsworthian or egotistical sublime; which is a thing per se and stands alone) it is not itself—it has no self— it is every thing and nothing—It has no character—it enjoys light and shade; it lives in gusto, be it foul or fair, high or low, rich or poor, mean or elevated—It has as much delight in conceiving an Iago as an Imogen. What shocks the virtuous philosopher, delights the camelion Poet. It does no harm from its relish of the dark side of things any more than from its taste for the bright one; because they both end in speculation. A Poet is the most unpoetical of any thing in existence; because he has no Identity—he is continually [informing] and filling some other Body . . . . When I am in a room with People if I ever am free from speculating on

---

[8] Letter to Bailey, November 22, 1817.

creations of my own brain, then not myself goes home to myself: but the identity of every one in the room begins to press upon me that I am in a very little time annihilated.[9]

True perception of essence, it is clear, requires something more than a subjective perceptual relationship; it must result from a fellowship with essence, and this fellowship comes about through an alchemy whereby the poet's identity is destroyed. In the ode, therefore, as Keats moved to a more intimate and self-obliterating relationship with the urn and the figures on it, so, proportionately, their apparent oppositions—chastity-marriage, deities-mortals, pursuit-escape, song-no tone—were blotting each other out; and the unselfed Keats was entering into a fellowship with their vital inwardness in which these oppositions are resolved. As his empathy with outward forms increases, so the elements of their outward conflicts converge and fuse to become their essence.

But what are the gradations of happiness that are "a regular stepping of the Imagination towards a Truth"? First,

> *Fold*
> *A rose leaf round thy finger's taperness,*
> *And soothe thy lips.*[10]

After this sensuous delight in nature,

> *hist, when the airy stress*
> *Of music's kiss impregnates the free winds,*
> *And with a sympathetic touch unbinds*
> *Eolian magic from their lucid wombs:*
> *Then old songs waken from enclouded tombs;*
> *Old ditties sigh above their father's grave;*
> *Ghosts of melodious prophecyings rave*
> *Round every spot where trod Apollo's foot;*
> *Bronze clarions awake, and faintly bruit,*
> *Where long ago a Giant Battle was;*

---

[9] Letter to Woodhouse, October 27, 1818.
[10] *Endymion*, I. 781-83.

[25]

And, from the turf, a lullaby doth pass
In every place where infant Orpheus slept.[11]

If we " feel " these things—the beauty of nature and of music—
or rather, if we can experience the essence of sensuous delights
and then perceive the essence of greater values through the penetrating power of the imagination,

> *that moment have we stept*
> *Into a sort of oneness, and our state*
> *Is like a floating spirit's. But there are*
> *Richer entanglements, enthralments far*
> *More self-destroying, leading, by degrees,*
> *To the chief intensity: the crown of these*
> *Is made of love and friendship, and sits high*
> *Upon the forehead of humanity.*
> *All its more ponderous and bulky worth*
> *Is friendship, whence there ever issues forth*
> *A steady splendour; but at the tip-top,*
> *There hangs by unseen film, an orbed drop*
> *Of light, and that is love: its influence,*
> *Thrown in our eyes, genders a novel sense,*
> *At which we start and fret; till in the end,*
> *Melting into its radiance, we blend,*
> *Mingle, and so become a part of it,—*
> *Nor with aught else can our souls interknit*
> *So wingedly: when we combine therewith,*
> *Life's self is nourish'd by its proper pith,*
> *And we are nurtured like a pelican brood.*[12]

v

The ode, I think, will now admit us into the presence of its
mystery. The steps of " the Imagination towards a Truth " are
the empathic entrances into rose leaf (the sensuous beauty of
nature), into music (essence imaginatively gained through the
medium of art), and into love (spiritual essence). And in the
ode a similar pleasure thermometer has dramatically been emerging

---

[11] *Ibid.*, 783-94.   [12] *Ibid.*, 795-815.

into vividness, ordering itself into the symbols of those three areas of the mutable world in which there is happiness because, although they are of this world, fellowship with their essence raises us beyond the misery of mutability by identifying us with " a sort of oneness," the mysterious core of life. Essence, however, is atemporal, whereas the pleasure thermometer, because it belongs to this side of heaven's bourne, is a chronological program of becoming. Since the ode is a poem of the atemporal, Keats must overcome the element of time implicit in the pleasure thermometer, and hence he transfers the sense of time to the reader's growing awareness, instead of introducing the symbols in a hierarchical sequence. The temporality now lies in the reader's becoming increasingly more conscious of the gradual unveiling of the symbols, all three of which may therefore emerge cotemporaneously. The frieze which contains the three symbols is thus as free from time as the heaven's bourne it symbolizes.

The corresponding symbols in the ode—trees, song, and lovers —lurk beneath the texture of the first stanza and are scattered; come to the surface in the second and are apportioned their relative significances, but remain in disorder. And in the third stanza they become discrete and dramatically fall into proper place. Each of the first two symbols, trees and song, is there housed in its own distinct two-line unit (in contrast to the uninterrupted flow of the first stanza), and each of the two-line units is sharply end-stopped to mark off the emphatic progression of the symbols:

> *Ah, happy, happy boughs! that cannot shed*
> *Your leaves, nor ever bid the Spring adieu;*
> *And, happy melodist, unwearied,*
> *For ever piping songs for ever new.*

The third symbol—the " orbed drop / Of light " which is love—is also housed in its own end-stopped unit, but the unit is appropriately extended to three lines (and is followed by an appendage to be considered shortly). The passage in *Endymion* makes it clear that the three symbols are not equally spaced on the pleasure thermometer, but that the first two are the means of entry into that vast range at the top of which is love; and the distribution of the lines in stanza three of the ode (2, 2, 3 +) corresponds to that difference. Since happiness lies *in* each symbol because we are full alchemized only by a self-destroying entrance *into* the symbol until we " Mingle, and so become a part of it," then each symbol is properly described as happy. But the highest of these intensities is therefore surrounded by a clustering repetition of the word and is, moreover, " *More* happy love! *more* happy, happy love! " In its Keatsian sense the repetition of " happy " conveys an empathic experience that is nervously taut.

In the first three stanzas there is also a drama of rhythms that coincides in its movement with that outward drama wherein the three symbols emerge from obscurity, grope about in the second stanza for a spiritual cosmos, and triumphantly secure a clear-cut, lucid order in the third. By this coincidence the rhythmical pattern also helps convey the significance of the more overt development of the images. First, the swelling tempo of the first stanza, accelerated by the staccato breaking of the questions, gives way to the slower harmony of the second, and then smoothes itself out in the orderly, sharply comparted phrasing of the third. The final sense of a controlled order in the third stanza is aided by the slow, deliberate movement that results from the clear ordonnance, from the repetition of " happy," and from the recurrence of the two patterns: "Ah, happy boughs . . . happy melodist . . . happy love," and " For ever piping . . . for ever new . . . For ever warm . . . For ever panting . . . for ever young." Second, the suggestion of disorder in the rhymes of the first sestet (cdedce) persists in those of the second (cdeced); but the sestet of the third stanza (cdecde) conveys the same sense of the unfolding of a spiritual harmony that is to be found in this stanza in the ordering of the symbols, the neat grouping of the rhetorical units, and the retarding of the tempo.

However, to read the first three stanzas only as a drama among the symbols, we have noted, is to see the drama in only one of its manifestations, for an implied drama between the poet and the symbols is also being unfolded, a drama that is conveyed by the mode of expression rather than by its substance. The evolution of the symbols is also the subtle involution of the poet. There are two of these empathic dramas being enacted in the first three stanzas. One, the self-destruction of the images in order that they may symbolize the dynamic stasis and the selflessness of heaven's bourne, quickly comes to a climax in the first stanza; the other, the unselfing of the poet by his entry into the unselfed symbols, occupies all three of the stanzas. The first of the two empathic movements centers about the word " ecstasy." We have already seen that, in the sense of " the most exquisite passion," the word tends, after the strenuous action of " pursuit " and " struggle," to draw together the mortal and immortal symbols toward a point of fusion so that in the next stanza the poet may move into an empathy with them and fix them in timeless activity. But in the sense of " the passage of the soul out of the self " ($\dot{\epsilon}\kappa + \iota\sigma\tau\dot{\alpha}\nu\alpha\iota$ = to make stand outside) it describes the consummation of the symbols' empathic act. That the word had this significance to Keats is clear from lines in the " Ode to a Nightingale ":

> *While thou art pouring forth thy soul abroad*
> *In such an ecstasy!*

The poet's own empathic advance is externalized, in part, by the contraction of his attention as it moves from the total urn in the opening lines, to the frieze on the urn, to the intense activity in the frieze. The sequence becomes organic instead of artificial

[29]

by the personification of the urn: "Thou still unravish'd bride." Because of the personification Keats can establish a quasi-human rapport with the urn, who can then introduce him to the persons on its frieze. "What men or gods are these?" he asks the personified urn, as he moves one degree into its inner existence. The apostrophe makes the urn a circle within the poet's circle; the question makes the two circles coincide. In the second stanza, no longer regarding the total urn, he addresses the symbols directly as he is enfolded still further into the core of the urn: "ye soft pipes, play on," "Fair youth . . . thou canst not leave / Thy song." He is now inside the frame of the urn, coincident with the figures of its frieze. Finally, in the third stanza he has fully entered into the dynamically static existence of the symbols themselves as he does not merely address them, but, by means of the ecstatic exclamations, participates in their sensations and experiences. The poet has become engaged not only in the urn, but also in the frieze, and even in the life of the figures themselves as the psychic distances are destroyed and art becomes reality. Indeed, the reality has become vicarious experience.

This empathic movement of the poet's consciousness from consideration of the urn as total object to a participation in the inwardness of the symbols also has a modal enactment so that it is conveyed not only by observable gestures but also by the verbal form in which those gestures are couched. Let us suppose a scale of grammatical moods arranged in order of the increasingly empathic relationships they establish between subject and predicate. The least empathic, the most remote, is the interrogative, since it only asks that some sort of nexus be formed between subject and predicate. The implication that something is not known makes that something distantly remote from the subject and places between subject and predicate the person questioned. This is the degree of the poet's separation from the symbols at the conclu-

sion of stanza one, especially as his questions have the air of
being rhetorical and promise never to be answered. The two next
more empathic moods are mingled in the second stanza. Here
the indicative ("Heard melodies are sweet," "thou canst not
leave / Thy song," etc.) implies that the subject has knowledge
of the predicate; and the imperative ("play on," "Pipe," "do not
grieve") assumes that the relationship is now so intimate that
the subject may impel the predicate to an action. These impera-
tives are further reinforced by the vocatives ("ye soft pipes,"
"Fair youth," "Bold Lover"), for the vocative is to the noun
as the imperative is to the verb. At the height of these empathic
moods is the exclamatory, for it assumes that the subject is
engaging in the life of the predicate—has mingled, "and so become
a part of it." Keats now experiences the happiness of the symbols
and knows, not objectively, but in his newly-acquired subjectivity,
that the boughs cannot shed their leaves and that the love is "For
ever warm and still to be enjoy'd." With the increasing intensities
of the pleasure thermometer there has been integrated proportionately a scale of modal intensities so that the subjective and the
objective intensities are correlated and made interdependent.

There is also a third aspect of the drama of the poet's absorption, in addition to the movement of his consciousness and the
modal forms in which the movement is expressed. This third is
a drama of grammatical subordination and independence. In the
first stanza, we have seen, the three symbols are in a subordinate
grammatical form or are subordinate to their full eventual semantic
values; in the second the symbols are in a clearly defined independent form and are related to oxymoronic conditions which are
expressed in equally independent form: "Heard melodies are
sweet, but those unheard / Are sweeter; therefore, ye soft pipes,
play on." But in the climactic third stanza Keats must enter into
heaven's bourne, not merely describe it objectively. He must

assimilate its nature in proportion as he enters more deeply into this region and consequently as its nature becomes more intimately a part of him. Therefore in the third stanza the statements of the nature of heaven's bourne slip from independent to subordinate form and thereby fall somewhat below the main level of conscious attention, just as the images themselves had been subliminal in the first stanza. " That cannot shed / Your leaves " is adjectival and is perceptible only through the independence of the image " boughs," and the same relationship applies to " For ever piping songs for ever new " and " melodist," " For ever warm and still to be enjoy'd " and " love." The conditions of heaven's bourne have been assimilated into the life of the symbols and of the poet, for at the height of the pleasure thermometer, as a consequence of the interknitting of the soul with essence,

> *Life's self is nourish'd by its proper pith,*
> *And we are nurtured like a pelican brood.*

Just as the legendary pelican partakes of the blood (essence) of its mother, who is physically distinct from her offspring although essentially the same, so through increasing intensities and enthrallments human life may ultimately be nourished in spirit by partaking of the nature of heaven's bourne, from which it is necessarily separated by that " fragile bar / That keeps us from our homes ethereal "[13] but to which human life belongs in its essential nature. What Keats has in mind is something approximately Eucharistic, and it is this Eucharistic act that is reflected in the adjectival absorption of the oxymoronic nature of heaven's bourne in stanza three.

The early part of this chapter sufficiently describes the third manifestation of the dramatic course in the first three stanzas— that is, the convergence of the mortal and immortal, or the

---

[13] *Ibid.*, 360-61.

Dionysian and Apollonian, to a point of interpenetration, along with the attendant deceleration of rhythms from the eager excitement of the first stanza to the slower harmony of the second and to the careful and neat deliberation of the third. But it must now be added that this is an insufficient account, for heaven's bourne is not a region of inertia, but of a stasis that at the same time is dynamic. Its immutability arises from an intensity of stress, not from the absence of it. And correspondingly, the leisurely pace and orderly grouping of the rhetorical units in stanza three are contained in exclamations, that is, in the most passionate and disorderly of the moods. The increasing Apollonian ordonnance that marks the emergence of the symbols out of their original obscurity and disorder, and the countercurrent of this increasing ordonnance—the increasing Dionysian intensity that marks the progress of the poet from mild wonderment to selfless ecstasy—have now come together at their climax. But here there is no clash between the dynamic and the static. There was such an opposition in the first stanza, for there the two qualities were conveyed by juxtaposed symbols seeking a reconciliation with each other. But as form and content always tend to absorb each other into an organic union, flux and stasis—the ecstatic content and the neat ordering—blend into a powerful tension in stanza three to reflect the Dionysian-Apollonian character of heaven's bourne.

Yet even this account does not fully describe Keats' amazingly complex treatment of the dynamic and the static, for he not only regulates the tempo of his rhythms to control the meaning of his poem, but also deals directly with the subject of time. It is especially pertinent that he do so, since the ideal condition towards which the first movement of the poem strives is one in which all the intense activities of the temporal world continue to exist, but outside the context of time. What Keats seeks is the steadfastness of the bright star, but not its "lone splendour"; instead, he aspires to be

> *still steadfast, still unchangeable,*
> *Pillow'd upon my fair love's ripening breast,*
> *To feel for ever its soft fall and swell,*
> *Awake for ever in a sweet unrest.*[14]

Towards this timeless and changeless intensity the deceleration of chronological time ("slow time") in the first stanza is moving. The second stanza then places the symbols at heaven's bourne and therefore in a context of an infinitude of time. Here this endless timefulness is conveyed in the manner in which it is intelligible to the mutable world of extensions: that is, by absolutely denying something's not continuing to exist. This is the construction of "thou canst not [ever] leave / Thy song," "nor ever can those trees be bare," and "She cannot [ever] fade." The three verbs (leave, be bare, fade), each one corresponding to one of the three central symbols, have to do with passage from earthly existence; and the negation of these verbs therefore creates an infinity of mutable or chronological time, an absolute extension of the time that passes. From the point of view of the world, infinitude is merely the denial of the finitude of earthly being. It appears that the poet is in the dimensional world contemplating heaven's bourne, and hence must translate its atemporality into dimensional concepts. However, in the last line of this stanza and in stanza three the poet has himself entered into the realm where time exists in its essence and therefore is without extension. This is the sense conveyed by the repetition of the boldly positive assertion "For ever": "For ever wilt thou love," "For ever piping songs for ever new," "For ever warm," "For ever panting, and for ever young." It is as though the double negatives of stanza two, denying

---

[14] "Bright star! would I were steadfast as thou art."

the cessation of worldly existence, constitute the only conceivable human definition of an infinite extension which in its repetition at heaven's bourne is known positively because it is without extension. The difference is that between infinite timefulness and the infinitude of absolute time. Into this extensionless time are assimilated the piping of the songs and the warmth and panting of the love, which cannot be conceived without reference to chronological time; and the fusion forms the nature of heaven's bourne, where the fall and swell of " love's ripening breast " is caught up in the immutability of the lone star. There, becoming and being are one.

The temporal theme we have been following is also subtly symbolized in the first three stanzas by means of the subject of love and the love-act. In stanza one, we have seen, the long-continued purity of the urn-bride was juxtaposed with the imminent ravishment of the virginal maidens to reveal that in the mutable world only the unvital can approach the timeless because, being itself without action, it is not touched by the destructiveness of the temporal act; and that the vital, even though it seeks to remain outside the framework of mutability, is, by being vital (and therefore mortal), in imminent danger of destruction by act, for in the temporal world action is always becoming its own past tense. Only the unvital can be immutable; the vital must pass. And the state the poem is moving towards is one of timeless vitality, an immortality of passion, an oxymoronic fusion of the urn and the maidens.

The conditions of the two images are then brought together in stanza two but are viewed from the perspective of the mutable world, just as the infinity of time was interpreted in terms of worldly extension: " She cannot fade, though thou hast not thy bliss " (19). The maiden is as vitally virginal as in stanza one, but now, time having been extended infinitely, she is also as unvitally unravished as the urn. But in the world of mutability

[35]

the normal consequence of having bliss is a fading; and therefore an immortality of passion, a virginal ravishment, can be conceived of only by paradoxically abrogating this normal causal relationship: *even though* the lover cannot enjoy the act of love, the maiden is an immortality of passion and he will love forever.

Finally, in the climactic third stanza the oxymoronic condition is consummated, both the temporal and atemporal conceptions of an immortality of passion being fused in the ambiguity of the line "For ever warm and still to be enjoy'd" (26). From the temporal point of view of the mortal world, the love is still (yet) *to be* enjoyed; the maiden is passionately vital because she has not yet been ravished, and the lover will love forever because he cannot have his bliss. From an atemporal point of view, the love is *still* (forever) to be enjoyed. The presence of both meanings in the ambiguity of the line fuses the temporal and the atemporal, the mortal and the immortal. No longer must the lover forego the kiss, as in stanza two, in order that the maiden be eternally fair and that he love forever. The enjoying is an act that occupies a timeless eternity, and yet paradoxically it is unaffected by time because it is yet to become a temporal act.

It has already been observed that although the drama of the first three stanzas has been separated here into three strands for the purpose of analysis, within the poem the three are coextential. The empathic involvement of the poet is only the dramatic emergence of the symbols seen from a bias; and the progress towards a condition of mystic oxymoron is itself the emergence of the symbols and the annihilation of the poet's identity. This triunity is finally captured at the climax of the entire movement in the density of the repeated word "happy" in stanza three. In one sense, the word is an account of heaven's bourne, for if the symbols are happy, then in them lies the power to beckon the ready mind "to fellowship divine, / A fellowship with essence," and therefore to free one from space—that mutable extension that characterizes this world although not heaven's bourne. Moreover, the symbols themselves are also happy in their having attained heaven's bourne, where ultimate happiness is to be found in an eternality of passionate experience. Yet, in the literal sense, of course, boughs cannot be happy except that by a pathetic fallacy, which is akin to empathy, Keats has transferred to them the " happiness " he experiences in participating in their perfect existence at heaven's bourne. Or, to accept Keats' own premises, the happiness is experienced by the poet by his entering into the life of the boughs, the happiness being an aspect of their existence. Thus, in this word all three manifestations of the drama are contained in their complete fulfillment.

vi

In the third stanza, then, the first major movement of the poem has clearly reached a climax beyond which it cannot go, for the third stanza has exhausted all the potentialities of this movement and has left nothing more to be said. The poet, ecstatically unselfed into the symbols, is now partaking of the essence of life. If the poem is to continue, it must take a different direction and therefore result in a different intention. But if the statement that beauty is truth is the total intention of the poem, then surely it is here that it belongs, and no where else. For this is what the poem has been saying up to this point.

Beauty, it must be clear, is not an abstraction, but a beauty so exquisitely sensory as to be the sensuous essence of beauty— an inner and experiential intensity, not a form. Keats, I am convinced, could understand beauty only phenomenalistically—only as the sensory quality of the piping of songs and the warmth and panting of the lover. What " truth " means here I prefer not to say, except in the terms of the poem itself, with the aid of some confirmation by Keats' own statements elsewhere, although I think the dramatic movement of the poem alone impels one to intuit the meaning clearly enough. Truth certainly is not to be grasped by " consecutive reasoning," [15] nor by an exertion of the will. One certainly cannot attain it by pursuing it as a goal: Dilke, Keats wrote, " will never come at a truth as long as he lives; because he is always trying at it." [16] Contrarily, then, truth is as much the reward of " negative capability "—the power to have no self—as the penetration into essence is; and this penetration into essence is the act of perceiving beauty. Therefore Keats held that " What the imagination seizes as Beauty must be truth— whether it existed before or not." [17] It was this experiential nature of truth that Keats had in mind when he wrote that " axioms in philosophy are not axioms until they are proved upon our pulses." [18] Finally, we will recall that the pleasure thermometer is " a regular stepping of the Imagination towards a Truth." If the perception of beauty and the perception of truth are fundamentally the same act, and if the sensory experiences of the pleasure thermometer lead not only to heaven's bourne, but also to truth, then beauty and truth are different in degree, not in kind, or are different conditions of the same thing.

Let us simply say, then, that beauty is the condition of being that extends up to heaven's bourne and includes it, and that truth is the condition of being that begins with heaven's bourne and continues beyond it. In heaven's bourne they meet, for there the sensory experience of beauty is divested of time, space, and identity, and therefore of all that makes it untrue in this world. When, consequently, we have seen it enacted in the ode that the love is " For ever warm and still to be enjoy'd," we might well conclude

[15] Letter to Bailey, November 22, 1817.
[16] Letter to George and Georgiana Keats, September 17–27, 1819.
[17] Letter to Bailey, November 22, 1817.
[18] Letter to Reynolds, May 3, 1818.

that therefore beauty is truth. That the aphorism is delayed until after the poem has taken a different direction should make us suspect that it has a somewhat different and less significant role to play in proportion as the remaining dramatic action qualifies the enactment in the first three stanzas of the fact that at heaven's bourne beauty is truth.

vii

The new direction taken by the action is not distinct from the first, but arises organically out of it, as antithesis arises out of thesis. Having gained full empathic entrance into essence, and having been carried by that essence to the height of the scale of intensities, Keats is at last able to experience a nature which is forever becoming and so cannot bid the Spring adieu, and song which is forever the same and yet forever new. His attaining the height—the orbed drop of light that is love—causes him to prolong his ecstasy beyond that aroused by nature and song: " For ever warm and still to be enjoy'd, / For ever panting, and for ever young." And Keats would continue in this fellowship with esssence—if he could. So long as he can conceive of heaven's bourne as an organic fusion—temporal warmth, enjoyment, panting, and youth that are caught up in atemporality—he may safely remain there in his vision.

But his next account of this area is a powerful drama of meaningful ambiguities whose struggle with each other eventually filters out the mortal from the immortal, the mutable from the immutable, beauty from truth. Fundamentally, it is a drama of syntax, for it appears that instead of continuing to coalesce opposites by absorbing one into another, Keats has stumbled into expressing the oxymoronic condition by opposing contraries: " All breathing human passion far above." The tendency of the reader's mind is to smooth out the syntax: the passion of the lovers, it half feels, is far above human passion and distinct from it. And yet Keats' intention is to say precisely that the love is " All breathing human passion far above," for this is the syntactical analogue of the mystic oxymoron. The love is indeed a human passion, and at the same time it is far above all mutable human passion, for at heaven's bourne mortal and immortal, the temporal and atemporal, beauty and truth, are one. The line corresponds in its oxymoronic syntax to Endymion's statement:

> *Now, if this earthly love has power to make*
> *Men's being mortal, immortal,*[19]

for here the adjacency of " mortal " and " immortal " brought about by the inversion " being mortal " is designed to deny the dichotomy of mortal and immortal and to convey instead the sense that although men's mortal being is made immortal by love, it thereby loses none of its mortal attributes except its mortality, its existence in a context of mutability and decay. But unlike the oxymoronic pattern of " For ever warm and still to be enjoy'd," which organically assimilates a temporal act into an atemporal texture through an ambivalence of meaning, the syntactical oxymoron is synthetic, for it is positional and therefore the meaningful inversion is ready to dissolve into a mere opposition of " human passion " and " far above." The fine coalescence of the antithetical conditions, one feels, is too strenuous for the merely conceptual mind to sustain, and it threatens to disintegrate upon the least incaution, even an incaution in choice of syntax.

At first glance, like the poet himself, we do not see that he has stumbled, for the line seems inevitable enough, and the words " human passion " appear in an inconspicuous position. But the line produces not only the meaningful ambiguity nicely calculated to express the fusion of the human and the superhuman, but also a certain degree of bewilderment, which the poet seems to share.

[19] *Endymion*, I. 843-44.

Could it mean that the passion is human and yet is far above that human passion that leaves a heart high-sorrowful? or that something far above human passion leaves a heart high-sorrowful? or that there is something far above human passion, and it is human passion which leaves a heart high-sorrowful? At any rate, the damage has been done, and out of the bewildering disintegration of the syntax comes an unexpected attention to merely human passions and the sobering recollection that they leave a " heart high-sorrowful and cloy'd, / A burning forehead, and a parching tongue." It appears that the poet has not created the confusion, but that the unstable situation his vision created has bewildered him in the midst of his ecstasy and forced him into a direction that he did not intend or expect. The recollection of the mortal world is calling him back to his sole self and is filtering out of heaven's bourne its component parts. On the one side is the immutability of " far above "; on the other are the agony and the impermanence attendant upon the experience of intensity in this world.

Out of this fracturing of heaven's bourne the next movement of the drama springs. Continuing to participate in the activity of the frieze, Keats now asks three questions. The first, like those of the first stanza, asks for identity: " Who are these coming to the sacrifice? " But of course there can be no answer, for at heaven's bourne there is only selflessness. The next two questions then introduce a new and significant element into the poem; they ask for directions: *to* what green altar is the sacrificial procession going? and *from* what town has it come? These are spatial questions and can no more be answered than those of identity, for heaven's bourne is essential space. The result of fellowship with essence is that we become " Full alchemiz'd, and free of space." It places man in the conditions of " truth " that Keats once experienced in the Lake District: after recording the date, he added, " I merely put *pro forma,* for there is no such thing as time and space, which by the way came forcibly upon me on seeing for the first hour the Lake and Mountains of Winander." [20]

The altar and town are therefore dimensional points as irrelevant to heaven's bourne as they are absent from the frieze. The procession itself is frozen in space and time on the urn: it can never arrive at the altar; it can never return to the town. It is poised between heaven and earth, and is the "element filling the space between." However, in the poet's mind the scene has now thawed and its frozen dimensions have begun to flow, for although the poet's attention is being concentrated on the spaceless procession, he is now imagining its before and after. The heaven's bourne of stanza three has been translated into the mutable world; the figures of the frieze have been extracted from the world of art and are being examined in the light of mutable reality. The symbols of the third stanza had acted in absolute time and space, but, mortal and immortal having now been separated out of heaven's bourne by the recollection of human passions, the poet sees the same procession in earthly, and therefore dimensional, space and time. In stanza three the theme had been that between doing and done lies the eternally vital act—the essence of growth, song, and love. In stanza four the theme is that at each moment in the extensional world, act is either doing or done. And the figures of the first three stanzas, when now observed in a spatial and temporal context, must expend their dynamic movement by having places from which to come and to which to go, a beginning and an end.

The priest who leads the procession is doubly mysterious: he is as much without identity as the other figures at heaven's bourne; and in addition he is to conduct a religious mystery. The sacrificial altar towards which the procession goes is, then, dedicated to heaven, to a realm of pure spirit: the immortal without the mortal,

[20] Letter to Thomas Keats, June 25-27, 1818.

truth without beauty. And the town that the souls leave is the town all souls leave in their human progress towards the heaven-altar. Only the dynamically static figures appear on the urn, only heaven's bourne is depicted there; but the now dimension-bound mind of the poet, no longer able to hold mortal and immortal in oxymoronic fusion, divides it imaginatively into its component symbols: the heaven-altar and the world-town. And he thrusts them to the opposite extremes of the scene. The component parts were also separate in stanza one as men and gods, chastity and marriage, quiet and ecstasy, but they were converging towards a union. In stanza four, however, the oppositions have been separated out only to move farther apart and become irreconcilable: the souls, having left the sensory realm in their journey to the heaven-altar, can never return to explain the world's desolation, its division from heaven's bourne, the impossibility of the soul's remaining eternally on earth. For in the mutable world in which the poet has now imaginatively enfolded the sacrificial procession, time and space create only one universal history: a passage of souls from the world-town to a heaven-altar, from which there is no return. At heaven's bourne all eternally is; in the mutable world, all passes. And therefore it cannot be from man's own total history that man will learn the purpose for which the soul must leave the world desolate. If he is to learn that purpose, it must be by other means.

Most of stanza four is devoted to the town, for the recollection of human passion is calling upon the poet to make a commentary upon the mortal world, not the realm of pure spirit. Yet, Keats does not hate the world for not being a heaven. To him it is the source of rich beauty, an opportunity for an enthrallment in the essence of the sensuous; and it differs from heaven in its condition of being, not in its kind. It must, then, be viewed with loving tenderness for what it is—and yet with pity for all it is not. The town, he emphasizes, is little; the word " street " sounds small against the spaceless sweep of the first three stanzas; unlike the men-gods, those eternal youths who have been the actors in the drama up to this point, the inhabitants are only humble " folk "; and " emptied " not only has a hollow and barren ring, but, like the word " little," underscores the spatial extension of the mutable world, in which it is possible to speak of size or to remove something and leave a void. Instead of the vital tension of selfless ecstasy at heaven's bourne, the self-enclosing and therefore antiempathic " citadel " is only " peaceful " in the solemnity of the " pious morn." The town is now desolate (ambiguously both " sad " and " alone ") because the soul has completely escaped the mortal form to leave a worldly desolation.

Moreover, the word " silent " works like a thread to integrate the stanza ironically with the rest of the poem. In stanza one, silence results from an amplitude of extension; by enduring in time, the urn is tending to draw thin the extensions of the world in which it exists and so is related to quietness, silence, and slow time. Because extensions seem not to affect the urn, in a sense it is without these extensions. But this silence has been introduced mainly to lead us to another kind in stanza two; here silence is the absolute of sound, its vital essence, which can be made audible only by adding to it the accidents of the dimensional world. In stanza four, however, we are fully back in the mortal world, where silence results only from the removal of sound. In stanza two, not to hear is to hear most essentially; now, not to hear is to have nothing to hear. The soul having withdrawn from physical matter, there is an everlasting void in sound, just as there is also a void in space: the streets for evermore will silent be. In the last stanza the thread of this theme will appear once again as the " silent form " of the urn when at last we have returned to a silence like that of the opening stanza. (But, we shall see, this final silence will, in the very act of completing the circle of this theme, take on a new and much larger meaning.)

Finally, the theme of time is also woven into stanza four in the words " for evermore " (38) and "[not] e'er " (40) to produce the same ironic inversion of meaning. In stanza two the atemporality of heaven's bourne was conceived in dimensional terms; negating the absence of dimension created an infinite dimension and thus a plenitude of chronological time. But in stanza three the atemporality was seen directly from heaven's bourne, and the sense of that essence of time was dinned into the reader's mind by the regular recurrence of the words " for ever." However, only not-being can truly be chronologically infinite in the mutable world, and it was for this reason that a complex periphrasis had been required in stanza two to express the chronological infinitude of essential being. At heaven's bourne Being itself—the essential " ditties of no tone "—exists in essential time; however, only the absence of sound can truly be eternal in the world. At heaven's bourne act never becomes done—" For ever wilt thou love " " though thou hast not thy bliss." But in the extensional world of stanza four, where only not-being can be infinite, everness can truly come only *after* the act is done: " and not a soul . . . can e'er return " and " thy streets for evermore / Will *silent* be."

Just as the progress toward heaven's bourne in the first three stanzas involved the gradual absorption of the poet's identity, so the fracturing and dispersion of the oxymoronic factors involve the retreat of the poet from the completely self-annihilating empathy of stanza three, until he is again contracted within his own citadel-like self. In one sense, the empathy is as great in stanza four as in stanza three, for the poet is still so greatly assimilated into the life and reality of the figures of the frieze that he can concern himself with their origin and destination; and the repetition in the sestet of stanza four of the orderly configuration of rhymes in stanza three (cdecde) suggests this relationship of the two stanzas. But the very act of placing the figures in a spatial context and of conceiving of them imaginatively in a framework more extensive than the frieze necessarily implies a degree of separation between the poet and the symbols. Consequently stanza four inverts the previous empathic direction and traces the return route from stanza three back to one. Although the return to the interrogative mood in stanza four suggests the empathic remoteness of stanza one, the poet is here questioning, not the urn, but no specific addressee; and hence, although the question " Who are these coming to the sacrifice? " divorces the poet from the figures, no barrier has yet been intruded between them. The poet has now withdrawn sufficiently so that he can next address the mysterious priest, one of the figures, and thereby he has retreated beyond the distance in stanza two, for the relationship of poet to figures is now merely that of subject to predicate, the priest standing between the two. Having sufficiently withdrawn from the figures inside the frieze to question one of them, he next arrives at a point midway between the frieze and the total urn, for the little town that he addresses, although an image provoked by the poet's participation in the activity within the frieze, exists only in his own imagination.

This movement then reaches its fulfillment in stanza five. There the poet has retreated fully from all engagement in the urn, is wholly self-contained, and is once again, as in stanza one, addressing the total personified urn: " Fair attitude " (i. e., beautiful pose). Proportionately as the poet withdraws, the figures in the frieze take on greater psychic distance. Once vitally engaged in a foreverness of passionate activity, they shrink from view as they are surrounded by the imagined symbols of town and altar, and finally in stanza five freeze to marble, become lifeless embroidery superimposed on the urn instead of dynamic values at the heart of the urn. And they therefore slip into the same subordinate grammatical position they occupied in stanza one: " *with* brede / Of marble men and maidens," " *With* forest branches and the trodden weed." The dissolution of the mystic oxymoron which is heaven's bourne, the descent of the symbols, and the retreat of the poet are, like their opposites, a single dramatic movement.

viii

We can now see the two major interlacing patterns of the ode. The first pattern makes the five stanzas perfectly symmetrical and brings the poem round full circle. The empathic progress, the evolution of the symbols, and the convergence upon heaven's bourne move forward in the first two stanzas; in the third and central stanza they all come to a climax and find the origin of their dissolution; and they fall away to their original condition in the remaining two, the full return of the circle being marked by the return in the last stanza to the rhyme-pattern of the first (cdedce). But this is only the formal orientation of the drama of the ode into the artistic neatness of perfect structural balance; and if we consider this complete circular movement alone, the drama seems to have taken us on a perilous journey only to return us to the point from which we started. We appear to have traveled to heaven's bourne only to return home and know that our journey was futile. Within this pattern, however, another is operative that gives the drama its meaning.

Like the first stanza, the fourth is made up largely of rhetorical questions; and the last stanza, like the third, is largely exclamatory; and into both stanzas four and five are absorbed declarative statements like those of three. It is as though, after the climax in stanza three, Keats were beginning the movement of the poem all over again; as though, having completed his independent clause in the first three stanzas, he were now qualifying it with a dependent clause which will have approximately the same rhetorical form as the independent clause but which will invert the direction of the symbols and the poet's empathy. This pattern suggests the two waves of the Italian sonnet, a form with which Keats had recently been experimenting, for the second wave, although weaker, is carried by the impetus of the first to a resolution the first could not attain. As the first movement dissolves beneath it, this second and briefer sweep of the poem, moving rhetorically in the same course as the first, will climb forward to find for the first movement its meaning.

ix

What, then, are we to make of the statement that beauty is truth, the statement incorporated into the exclamations of stanza five, just as there is a statement nestled among the questions of stanza four? The first three stanzas have acted out a vitality that is eternal, a passionate foreverness, a beauty that is truth. But we have already seen these conditions disintegrate in stanza four into a complete separation of world and spirit as the poet withdrew his self into the mortal and dimensional world. Having slipped back into only mortal comprehension and thereby having extended his consciousness around essence to embrace the spatial and temporal aspects of an eternity of passion—aspects which he sees as the symbolic town and altar—the poet has concluded stanza four with an assertion that contradicts the first three stanzas: the " streets for evermore / Will silent be; and not a soul to tell / Why thou art desolate, can e'er return." From the perspective of this world, spirit deserts the passionate existence; passion is mortal, and immortality does not embrace our sensory world. To put it bluntly, stanza three has said that at heaven's bourne beauty is truth; and stanza four has said that in this world beauty is not truth, truth is not beauty. If there is to be a consistent meaning in the poem, it must appear in a synthesis that reconciles the thesis of the first three stanzas and the antithesis in stanza four.

Surely, then, it cannot be the total intent of the poem to reveal merely that beauty is truth at heaven's bourne, for in stanza four the poem has said more than this. Nor, assuming now that the intention comprehends all of the last two lines of the poem, can it be the purpose to say that the sum total of earthly wisdom is the knowledge that beauty is truth at heaven's bourne and that this knowledge is sufficient. What the poem has been acting out is that this is the maximum wisdom, not the minimal—a bare sufficiency. Moreover, to know that beauty is identical with truth is not worldly wisdom, for the identity is a condition that does not exist here; and the knowledge therefore can be of no immediate aid within the confines of this life. Nor can it be that the identification of beauty and truth is an *experience* that embraces all the knowledge available to man *on earth*, a higher wisdom, presumably, being accessible hereafter; this is considerably more, not less, than stanza three admits, and it has been denied symbolically in stanza four. What is meant must be several removes from this, and in the opposite direction. If man is to " know " that beauty is truth, he must learn it, not by direct experience, but indirectly; it must be told him by the urn (" to whom thou say'st "), for otherwise he could not know it, since it is not true of the sphere of his direct experience and since no soul ever returns to tell the purpose for which the soul must abandon the mortal sphere. But the urn can divulge that purpose.

The intention of the poem, therefore, must be to hold up art as the source of the highest form of wisdom. It is in this more embracing sense, in addition to those we have already examined, that the urn has become in the final stanza a silent form which, although silent, paradoxically speaks to man. The very bourne of heaven does not noisily cry out to man its existence; knowledge of its nature is forever available, but man can gain it only by a self-annihilating entrance into the bourne itself. He may learn of the region of mystic oxymoron by being drawn into it, not by a direct communication of the mystery to him:

> *. . . there are throned seats unscalable*
> *But by a patient wing, a constant spell,*
> *Or by ethereal things that, unconfin'd,*
> *Can make a ladder of the eternal wind,*
> *And poise about in cloudy thunder-tents*
> *To watch the abysm-birth of elements.*
> *Aye, 'bove the withering of old-lipp'd Fate*
> *A thousand Powers keep religious state,*
> *In water, fiery realm, and airy bourne;*
> *And, silent as a consecrated urn,*
> *Hold sphery sessions for a season due.*
> *Yet few of these far majesties, ah, few!*
> *Have bared their operations to this globe—*
> *Few, who with gorgeous pageantry enrobe*
> *Our piece of heaven. . . .*
> *. . . every sense*
> *Filling with spiritual sweets to plenitude.*[21]

There are, Keats is saying, forces outside the range of mutability which are nevertheless perceptible in the texture of sensory things. These powers do not obtrude their meaning upon us, but, " silent as a consecrated urn, / Hold sphery sessions for a season due," for their very silence is pregnant with meaning. When through the ecstatic and visionary loss of his self one can mount the ladder of " ethereal things " and thereby participate in these silent sessions, his every sense is filled " with spiritual sweets to plenitude ": he experiences, that is, the sensory spirituality, the mortal immortality, the beauty-truth of heaven's bourne. The most meaningful form of communication results from a meeting of essence with essence and a passage of one into the other, not from a transfer of knowledge. " Man should not dispute or assert," Keats wrote to Reynolds, " but whisper results to his neighbour and thus

---

[21] *Endymion*, III. 23-39.

by every germ of spirit sucking the sap from mould ethereal every human might become great." [22] It is because the physical arts are less assertive than poetry and engage us directly in a sense-spirit experience instead of communicating and interpreting the experienced act that, I judge, the urn can tell its tale " more sweetly than our rhyme " (that is, than this poem, the ode), just as the assertive " heard melodies " are less sweet than those unheard. One of the grandeurs of immortality, Keats wrote, is that " there will be no space and consequently the only commerce between spirits will be by their intelligence of each other—when they will completely understand each other—while we in this world merely comprehend each other in different degrees." [23]

This spiritual communication is the meaningful silence that Keats attributes to the urn; a communication not fashioned into the noisiness of verbalization or conceptualization, but the silence with which the inwardness of the urn, one of the " thousand Powers," communicated to the poet in stanza three of the ode the nature of heaven's bourne and filled his every sense " with spiritual sweets to plenitude "—intensified sensuous beauty until it became also " spiritual " truth. The urn, indeed, did not directly communicate at all, but allowed the unindividualized self of the poet to come into the presence of its mystery, into one of its " sphery sessions." In the simplest terms, then, art does not communicate by thrusting its meaning upon the observer but by absorbing him into a participation in its essence:

> We hate poetry that has a palpable design upon us—and if we do not agree, seems to put its hand in its breeches pocket. Poetry should be great and unobtrusive, a thing which enters into one's soul, and does not startle it or amaze it with itself, but with its subject.—How beautiful are the retired flowers!

---

[22] Letter to Reynolds, February 19, 1818.
[23] Letter to George and Georgiana Keats, December 16, 1818–January 4, 1819.

how would they lose their beauty were they to throng into the highway crying out, " admire me I am a violet!—dote upon me I am a primrose! " [24]

Finally, art succeeds in drawing us into its essence—and thus in communicating—by teasing us " out of thought / As doth eternity " (44–45), for thought deals only with what is humanly conceivable and therefore limits one to the mutable world. Pan, we recall, is

> the unimaginable lodge
> For solitary thinkings; such as dodge
> Conception to the very bourne of heaven,
> Then leave the naked brain.

To enter into heaven's bourne we must circumvent the gravitational force of the conceptual mind, which would reduce the unimaginable to the imaginable, the unknown to the known. Yet, the silent communication of the essence of art teases us only out of thought; it does not substitute a different order of materials for those to which the conceptual mind is adequate. For heaven's bourne is made of the materials of conception existing under conditions that are beyond conception. Therefore, Keats once planned to write

> All that was for our human senses fitted.
> Then the events of this wide world I'd seize
> Like a strong giant, and my spirit teaze
> Till at its shoulders it should proudly see
> Wings to find out an immortality.[25]

He would not transcend the events of this wide world, but would strain to lift them into the immortality that begins at heaven's bourne to see them *sub specie aeternitatis*; he would see beauty as truth. Art, then, silently communicates by teasing us out of thought, in the sense that it raises the substance of thought beyond the dimensional restrictions of thought. It opens up the mystery that

[24] Letter to Reynolds, February 3, 1818.
[25] " Sleep and Poetry," 80-84.

is the core of life since " no great minist'ring reason "—conception—

> *sorts*
> *Out the dark mysteries of human souls*
> *To clear conceiving.*[26]

x

In this theory of the urn's silent communication of spiritual sweets through the poet's entrance into its sphery sessions is also to be found the heart of Keats' system of symbolism. Clearly, Keats did not believe the world itself to be symbolic; it is not an imperfect shadow of the real, where all values reside, nor is it the language in which God speaks directly to man. Hence its silence. But things of " water, fiery realm, and airy bourne " may become symbolic by a transfiguring act of the percipient which leads him into the presence of their essence, where the " Powers keep religious state." All things, then, may be symbolic in proportion to the intensity with which one is engaged in them, for this sensuous intensity is the magic that opens the husk of natural objects to the core and reveals their spiritual essences.[27] Every mental pursuit, Keats wrote,

> takes its reality and worth from the ardour of the pursuer— being in itself a nothing—Ethereal thing[s] may at least be thus real, divided under three heads—Things real—things semireal—and no things. Things real—such as existences of Sun Moon & Stars and passages of Shakspeare. Things semi-real such as Love, the Clouds &c which require a greeting of the Spirit to make them wholly exist—and Nothings which are made Great and dignified by an ardent pursuit—which by the by stamps the burgundy mark on the bottles of our Minds, insomuch as they are able to " *consec[r]ate whate'er they look upon.*" [28]

---

[26] *Ibid.*, 288-90.
[27] " The Poet " ("At morn, at noon, at Eve, and Middle Night ").
[28] Letter to Bailey, March 13, 1818.

Real things—boughs, a nightingale, an urn—become ethereal things, symbolic things, by the mind's hallowing act which disengages them from time and space and intensifies them until they are seen as the mortal-immortal, the beauty-truth, which is the mystery that permeates all things and gives them their meaning. The purpose of poetry is to capture things in their " etherial existence," which is divulged to the poet by his visionary journeys heavenward. When, for example, Keats was in the Lake District, he wrote, " I shall learn poetry here and shall henceforth write more than ever, for the abstract endeavor of being able to add a mite to that mass of beauty which is harvested from these grand materials, by the finest spirits, and put into etherial existence for the relish of one's fellows." [29] He would, that is, translate beauty into the conditions of " truth."

Truth and beauty, or the spiritual and the sensuous, are, then, different only in mode and not in kind, and intensity of experience at some ultimate point etherealizes the sensuous (the condition of the mortal world) into the spiritual (the condition of the immortal). " A melodious passage in poetry," wrote Keats, " is full of pleasures both sensual and spiritual. The spiritual is *felt* when the very letters and points of charactered language show like the hieroglyphics of beauty; the mysterious signs of our immortal freemasonry!" [30] It is for this reason that a " Life of Sensations "—of experiential intensities—is " ' a Vision in the form of Youth ' a Shadow of reality to come." [31] Thus the pleasure thermometer is also a scale of ethereal things. For nature or song or love does not have a value in itself; their values come into being by the passionate self-involvement of the percipient until his soul interknits with their core. They are a scale of ethereal things because they successively

[29] Letter to Thomas Keats, June 25-27, 1818.
[30] " On Edmund Kean as a Shakespearian Actor."
[31] Letter to Bailey, November 22, 1817.

evoke an increasingly more ardent pursuit until the pursuer is
nourished by life's proper pith; for the "ethereal things,"

> *unconfin'd,*
> *Can make a ladder of the eternal wind,*
> *And poise about in cloudy thunder-tents*
> *To watch the abysm-birth of elements.*[32]

These "ethereal things" which lead to the abysm-birth of elements—the mystery—are obviously also a pleasure thermometer of
real things and semireal things and no things transfigured by the
intensity with which they are experienced. And it is noticeable that
they are unconfined, abstracted from time and space by the ardor
of pursuit. The urn, then, is also made to become an ethereal thing,
for in itself it is only one of the "Things real," but it is pursued
with increasing ardor throughout the first three stanzas until the
poet is fully enthralled by its essence—the a-dimensional dynamic-
static being in its frieze—and thus is admitted into the sphery sessions of the Power available through all beauty. The first three
stanzas are a symbolizing, an etherealizing, of the urn, and hence a
progress to heaven's bourne. The life on the frieze is experienced
with such sensuous intensity (mad pursuit, wild ecstasy) that by
the third stanza it becomes the mysterious sign of "our immortal
freemasonry." But the force that makes the symbol is in the poet,
not in the urn; the urn can only beckon and incite the pursuit into
its essence. Thus, the formation of symbols is a creative act, not a
discovery. It is not the act of making essence presence—of finding
a shape to embody a value—but of making presence essence—of
seeing things under the immortal conditions that prevail at heaven's
bourne.

Etherealizing real things and nothing by intensity—or, as he
wrote in "Sleep and Poetry," seizing the events of the world and

[32] *Endymion*, III. 25-28.

then teasing his spirit until it has wings " to find out an immortality "—was more than a system of poetic symbolization to Keats. It was his religion. The account of ethereal things in the letter to Bailey follows hard upon Keats' admission to the orthodox Bailey that his own religious views are not those customarily held. And Keats had written Haydon earlier that the total plan of his life is

> the looking upon the Sun the Moon the Stars, the Earth and its contents as materials to form greater things—that is to say ethereal things—but here I am talking like a Madman greater things that [i. e., than] our Creator himself made!! [33]

The odes on the urn and the nightingale, " La Belle Dame Sans Merci," and " The Eve of St. Agnes " were religious experiences almost terrifying to their maker.

xi

The tangent along which the description of the urn as a silent form has led us will also help us to understand why the urn is a " sylvan historian." History is normally an account of persons, places, dates, and deeds; it has to do with the transitoriness of the world of dimensions and identities. And yet, when the poet asks for the identities of the figures, the name of the town, the location of the altar, and the particularities of the struggle and escape, the urn makes no answer. In the sort of history that provides answers for such questions Keats saw little value:

> *Hence, pageant history! hence, gilded cheat!*
> *Swart planet in the universe of deeds!* [34]

Records of intensely passionate moments in narratives created by imaginative insight—Juliet leaning

---

[33] Letter to Haydon, May 10-11, 1817.
[34] *Endymion*, II. 14-15.

Amid her window-flowers,—sighing,—weaning
Tenderly her fancy from its maiden snow,
                    . . . the silver flow
Of Hero's tears, the swoon of Imogen,
Fair Pastorella in the bandit's den

—these are the subject of true history.

The woes of Troy, towers smothering o'er their blaze,
Stiff-holden shields, far-piercing spears, keen blades,
Struggling, and blood, and shrieks—all dimly fades
Into some backward corner of the brain [35]

because these are outward events knowable in their entirety to the
senses and existing only in a context of time and space. They
belong to mutability and have not been lifted by a giant into an
immortality, or pursued with an ardor until they are " unconfined "
by space, time, and identity; they are " real things," not " ethereal
things," symbols. In Shakespeare's historical plays, the poetry,
unlike symbols " unconfined,"

is for the most part ironed and manacled with a chain of
facts, and cannot get free; it cannot escape from the prison
house of history, nor often move without our being disturbed
with the clanking of its fetters. The poetry of Shakespeare
is generally free as is the wind—a perfect thing of the elements, winged and sweetly coloured. Poetry must be free!
It is of the air, not of the earth; and the higher it soars the
nearer it gets to its home. The poetry of " Romeo and Juliet,"
of " Hamlet," of " Macbeth," is the poetry of Shakespeare's
soul—full of love and divine romance. It knows no stop in
its delight, but " goeth where it listeth "—remaining, however,
in all men's hearts a perpetual and golden dream. The poetry
of " Lear," " Othello," " Cymbeline," &c., is the poetry of
human passions and affections, made *almost ethereal by the
power of the poet.*[36]

---

[35] *Ibid.*, 8-11.
[36] Keats' essay " On Kean in ' Richard Duke of York.' " Italics mine.

Herein lies the difference between "pageant" history and "sylvan" history. The first particularizes and hence confines deeds to the mortal world, where everything is transitory. But "sylvan" history seizes human passions and makes them "almost ethereal by the power of the poet," which lifts them out of the dimensional and makes them the essence with which the soul may interknit. The difference is that between history and symbol—between an account of events in a world to which souls can never return to tell why the town is desolate, and an account of a realm where songs are forever new. Human history chronicles mutable becoming; but the urn is the essential historian and chronicles the essence of becoming, which is being, and therefore is not limited to time, place, and identity. Hence, although it cannot identify the pipes and timbrels of the world, it does chronicle the act which, by never becoming done, can never be recorded in "pageant" history.

xii

To return now to the concluding lines of the ode. Although the urn is able to reveal to man a oneness of beauty and truth, it is not able to inform him that this is the sum total of his knowledge on earth and that it is sufficient for his earthly existence ("all ye need to know"); for obviously he knows other things on earth, such as the fact that in the world beauty is not truth, and this should be even more valuable within the world than the knowledge that the two are one at heaven's bourne. But more important, the symbolic action of the drama at no point justifies the urn's limiting its message; nowhere has the urn acted out the fact that man knows no more on earth than this identity of beauty and truth, and that this knowledge is sufficient.

Now, it is significant that this is an ode *on* a Grecian urn. Had Keats meant *to*, he would have said so, as he did in the "Ode to a Nightingale." There the meaning of the poem arises out of the dramatic relations of the poet and the symbol; but *on* implies a commentary, and it is Keats who must make the commentary on the drama that he has been observing and experiencing within the urn. It is the poet, therefore, who speaks the words, " that is all / Ye know on earth, and all ye need to know," and he is addressing himself to man, the reader. Hence the shift of reference from " thou " (urn) to " ye " (man). I do not feel the objection frequently raised that if the last line and a half belong to the poet and are addressed to the reader, they are not dramatically prepared for. The poet has gradually been obtruding himself upon the reader's consciousness in the last two stanzas by withdrawing from his empathic experience and taking on identity. He has become distinctly present in the last stanza as a speaker addressing the urn, and proportionately the urn has shrunk from the center of dramatic interest; it is now but a short step for him to turn his address from urn to reader. Moreover, the reader has also been subtly introduced into the stanza, for the poet vividly marks his complete severance from the urn's essence by pluralizing himself (" tease us," " other woe / Than ours ") and thus putting himself into a category wholly distinct from the urn; and by this act Keats has now involved the reader as a third member of the drama. Finally, when the reader has been filtered out of the plural " us " and " ours " by the reference to " man " (48), the poet may now address to him his final observations on the drama.

But the poet is no more justified than the urn would be in concluding that the sum of necessary earthly wisdom is the identity of beauty and truth. Certainly when he returned to the dimensional world in stanza four he found the two to be antithetical, not identical. Something of the difficulty Keats encountered in trying to orient his meaning is to be seen in the three versions of the final lines that have manuscript or textual authority. Keats' manuscript and the transcripts made by his friends read,

Beauty is truth, truth beauty,—that is all. . . .

In the *Annals of the Fine Arts* for 1820, where the poem was first published, the line appears as

Beauty is Truth, Truth Beauty.—That is all. . . .

And the 1820 volume of Keats' poems reads,

" Beauty is truth, truth beauty,"—that is all. . . .

No one of these solves the problem, although each hints at the difficulty. Clearly each one strives to separate the aphorism from the following assertion by the poet; and at the same time each attempts to preserve a relation between the pronoun " that " and *something* that has gone before. Then, since we have seen that the antecedent of " that " cannot reasonably be the aphorism—since neither urn nor poet can be saying that all man knows and needs to know on earth is that beauty is truth—its antecedent must be the entire preceding sentence.

All that man knows on earth, and all he needs to know is that

When old age shall this generation waste,
Thou [the urn] shalt remain, in midst of other woe
Than ours, a friend to man, to whom thou say'st,
Beauty is truth, truth beauty.

Only this meaning can be consistent with the dramatic action of the poem, for it not only does not deny that in the world beauty is not truth, but also assimilates that fact into a greater verity. The sum of earthly wisdom is that in this world of pain and decay, where love cannot be forever warm and where even the highest pleasures necessarily leave a burning forehead and a parching tongue, art remains, immutable in its essence because that essence is captured in a " Cold Pastoral," a form which has not been created for the destiny of progressing to a heaven-altar, as warm and passionate man is. This art is forever available as " a friend to man," a power

willing to admit man to its " sphery sessions." The urn fulfills its
friendship as the comedies and tragedies of Beaumont and Fletcher
do, for, being the earthly souls of the dramatists, they, too,

> *Teach us, here, the way to find you,*
> *Where your other souls are joying,*
> *Never slumber'd, never cloying.*

They give us, that is, a prefigurative vision of a realm

> *Where the nightingale doth sing*
> *Not a senseless, tranced thing.*
> *But divine melodious truth;*
> *Philosophic numbers smooth;*
> *Tales and golden histories*
> *Of heaven and its mysteries.*[37]

The great end of poetry, Keats wrote, is " that it should be a
friend / To sooth the cares, and lift the thoughts of man," [38] for
art (unlike man, who cannot return to tell us of his postmortal
existence) allows a glimpse into that region which shows the full
meaning of those experiences which now produce only mortal
suffering, divulges the end for which they are destined, and so
eases the burden of the mystery. And art eases this burden by
holding out to man the promise that somewhere—at heaven's
bourne, where the woes of this world will be resolved—songs are
forever new, love is forever young, human passion is " human
passion far above," beauty is truth; that, although beauty is not
truth in this world, what the imagination seizes as beauty must be
truth—whether it existed before or not.

The knowledge that in art this insight is forever available is the
height of earthly wisdom; and it is all man needs to know, for it

---

[37] " Bards of Passion and of Mirth."
[38] " Sleep and Poetry," 245-57.

endows his earthly existence with a meaning and a purpose. It provides him with " A hope beyond the shadow of a dream." [39]

> . . . *thou must wander far*
> *In other regions, past and scanty bar*
> *To mortal steps, before thou cans't be ta'en*
> *From every wasting sigh, from every pain,*
> *Into the gentle bosom of thy love.*
> *Why it is thus, one knows in heaven above.*[40]

Or, like Keats, one may learn why by attending a sphery session of a Grecian urn.

---

[39] *Endymion*, I. 857.   [40] *Ibid.*, II. 123-28.

La Belle Dame Sans Merci

A Ballad

I

O what can ail thee, knight-at-arms,
  Alone and palely loitering?
The sedge has wither'd from the lake,
  And no birds sing.

II

O what can ail thee, knight-at-arms!
  So haggard and so woe-begone?
The squirrel's granary is full,
  And the harvest's done.

III

I see a lilly on thy brow,
  With anguish moist and fever dew,
And on thy cheeks a fading rose
  Fast withereth too.

IV

I met a lady in the meads,
  Full beautiful—a faery's child,
Her hair was long, her foot was light,
  And her eyes were wild.

V

I made a garland for her head,
  And bracelets too, and fragrant zone;
She look'd at me as she did love,
  And made sweet moan.

VI

I set her on my pacing steed,
  And nothing else saw all day long,

For sidelong would she bend, and sing
   A faery's song.

VII

She found me roots of relish sweet,
   And honey wild, and manna dew,
And sure in language strange she said—
   ' I love thee true.'

VIII

She took me to her elfin grot,
   And there she wept, and sigh'd full sore,
And there I shut her wild wild eyes
   With kisses four.

IX

And there she lulled me asleep,
   And there I dream'd—Ah! woe betide!
The latest dream I ever dream'd
   On the cold hill side.

X

I saw pale kings and princes too,
   Pale warriors, death-pale were they all;
They cried—' La Belle Dame sans Merci
   Hath thee in thrall!'

XI

I saw their starved lips in the gloam,
   With horrid warning gaped wide,
And I awoke and found me here,
   On the cold hill's side.

XII

And this is why I sojourn here,
   Alone and palely loitering,
Though the sedge has wither'd from the lake,
   And no birds sing.

La Belle Dame Sans Merci

$\mathcal{I}$T WOULD be difficult in any reading of Keats' ballad not to be enthralled by the haunting power of its rhythm, by its delicate intermingling of the fragile and the grotesque, the tender and the weird, and by the perfect economy with which these effects are achieved. Snared by the sensuous workings of the poem, one is greatly tempted to evaluate it entirely as a poem whose function is not the expression of human values, but whose end is attained when it fulfills its own stylistic requirements. Nevertheless, out of the dim sense of mystery and incompleteness that its artistry arouses there rise not only richly suggestive overtones, but also dark hints of a meaning that might be available to us could we penetrate its mystery. The imagination, for example, seizes upon the sedge that has withered from the lake and upon the absence of the birds' song, and elaborates the pictorial connotations of these stark images into all barren and desolate autumnal scenes that ever were. And yet, one senses an insufficiency in these affective and image-making energies of the poem, for the overtones also drive the mind to ask questions of conceptual intent. What, one wonders, is the larger meaning couched within the absence of song? why a knight-at-arms and an elfin grot? and what are the significances of the cold hill side and the pale warriors?

Nor are these probings of the mind without justification, since the poem contains within itself the power of compelling us to such questions. For Keats' symbolism is almost always dynamic. His poetry does not lie inert, waiting, like the poetry of Blake and some of the early work of Yeats, to yield itself up to a symbolic reading. Such poetry as theirs assumes that the world is symbolic, and therefore that if the poet selects images of symbolic import and orders them into an artistic intertexture that corresponds to the meaningful relationships in the cosmos, he has created a symbolic poem, let the reader read it as he will. However, we have seen that Keats' world is not symbolic; it is his vision of the world that is symbolic, and a greeting of the spirit is required to transmute image into symbol. Since " every mental pursuit takes its reality and worth from the ardour of the pursuer—being in itself a nothing," Keats must entice a pursuit of his images by the reader, whose ardor will transform them into symbols, " ethereal things."

In the ballad, therefore, Keats not only dramatized a myth, but also dramatized the fact that the narrative and its component images are symbolic. The first three stanzas are introductory in that they are addressed by an anonymous someone to the knight-at-arms, whose answer will then constitute the narrative body of the poem. These three stanzas consequently serve to set the story of the knight's adventures in an additional narrative framework, a dialogue between the knight and the stranger, with whom the reader tends to identify himself; and thus the reader is drawn more intimately into the knight's experiences, for he feels himself to be present as the knight speaks in his own person. But even more important, in the introductory stanzas images and human values are gradually blended stereoscopically until at length the reader's mode of poetic vision has been adjusted to see the symbolized value as the third-dimensional projection of the image.

The first two stanzas have identical patterns: the first half of each addresses a question to the knight-at-arms about his spiritual condition; and the second half comments on the natural setting. The similarity of the gaunt, pale appearance of the solitary knight to the desolation and decay of nature is clearly implied, but the absence of any explicit relationship leaves the connection vague and therefore fluid enough so that nature and the knight may later be welded into an organic, instead of a synthetic, union—a method reminiscent of the first stanza of the " Ode on a Grecian Urn." The second half of each of these stanzas is built around a coordination of two natural images (sedge and birds, the squirrel's granary and the harvest) ; and it is noticeable that the first pair are the natural images themselves, while the second are the materials of nature as shaped and molded by creatures for themselves. The progress is toward a closer integration of nature and man: the granary and the harvest are what creatures make of nature for their own use. Corresponding to these pairs of images are two pairs of adjectives in the halves describing the knight, the first pair exactly paralleling the natural images: alone, no birds sing ; palely loitering, the sedge has withered. All these balanced details, equally distributed to nature and the knight, now coalesce in the third stanza.

This stanza takes its structure from that of the second halves of the first two stanzas, for its pattern, too, depends upon the coordination of two natural images, lily and rose, and each image dominates half of the stanza, just as each image in the first two stanzas governs a single line. In other words, the structure of the third stanza is precisely that of the second halves of the first two, expanded to the length of a full stanza. The subject matter of the third stanza, however, is not the appearance of nature, but the spiritual condition of the knight-at-arms, which has been the theme of the first halves of the first two stanzas. By this absorption of the knight into the structural pattern of the natural imagery, the movement from a suggested but unstated relationship of man and nature in stanza one to an implied interrelationship in stanza two has now been completed. In the third stanza the two terms are organically integrated, and human values and natural images have been molded into interchangeable expressions: the lily and the rose are present in the knight's countenance, and his withering is theirs. This structural drama of their coalescence now compels a symbolic reading of the poem, and we cannot well avoid questioning the human relevance of the garlands, the elfin grot, and the cold hill side. If, to use Coleridge's definition, a symbol " partakes of the reality which it renders intelligible," the work of the first three stanzas is to make the symbols a living part of that reality.

ii

The first three stanzas, which make dramatic the subsequent narrating and excite a symbolic reading, introduce nine precisely balanced stanzas containing the main narrative (4–12). The progress of the knight in the first four (4–7) comes to a climax in the central one (8) when he is taken into the elfin grot, and in the last four (9–12) he withdraws from the grot. The withdrawal brings the poem back to the scene with which it began, the completion of the circular movement being marked by the fact that the last stanza echoes the first.

Whatever the specific source may have been, the narrative clearly belongs to a folk legend best known in the form of the mediaeval ballad " Thomas Rymer." In the version available to Keats in Robert Jamieson's *Popular Ballads*, 1806 (the variant in Scott's *Minstrelsy* differs in a few important details), Thomas encounters a beautiful lady whom he thinks to be the Queen of Heaven, but who identifies herself as " the queen of fair Elfland." She takes him upon her milk-white steed, for he must serve her for seven years; and for forty days and nights they ride through blood while Thomas sees neither sun nor moon. Forbidden to touch the fruit of this strange country lest he suffer the plagues of hell, Thomas eats the loaf and drinks the claret that the elf-queen has brought. At length they rest before a hill, and the elf-queen, placing his head on her knee, shows him three wonders—the roads to wickedness, to righteousness, and to fair Elfland. It is the last of these that they are to follow, and for seven years " True Thomas on earth was never seen." The relations of this narrative to a story of a knight-at-arms carried by a fairy's child to an elfin grot are too obvious to underscore. Apparently the myth of a journey to a mysterious otherworld that is neither heaven nor hell nor earth, and of capture there by the fairy magic of love for one who seems to be " Queen of Heaven," constituted a pattern that evoked from Keats a body of speculation ripe for expression and helped give these speculations an artistic shape.

Keats did not simply recast this folk legend into another artistic form but molded it into an expression of his deepest and most vivid conceptions. The legend was not merely an esthetic design that he felt he could bring closer to his idea of literary perfection; to him it was also a meaningful narrative in which he recognized his own journeys heavenward. Since, then, the substance of the folk ballad constitutes mainly the raw materials of Keats' creation, his modifications of the legend and his additions to it are the more obvious clues to his motives. It is noticeable that nearly all the larger narrative elements of the first four stanzas of Keats' central narrative (4–7) are present in the folk ballad also: the meeting with a fairy lady of great beauty, the implication of the lady's desire for Thomas, their sharing the pacing steed, and the knight's eating of the magic food. To these Keats has added three major details that do not appear in the folk ballad, even by implication: the knight weaves for the fairy's child a garland, bracelets, and a girdle of flowers; the lady sings " A faery's song "; and at length " in language strange she said— / ' I love thee true.' "

What Keats has woven into the narrative, it appears, is another version of the pleasure thermometer, a series of increasing intensities that absorb the self into essence: nature, song, and love. We have already seen the important role of the pleasure thermometer in the " Ode on a Grecian Urn," and we shall have occasion to see how functional it is in other poems of Keats. It was " a regular stepping of the Imagination towards a Truth," towards that beauty-truth which was his heart's desire, and each aspiration towards it carried him along the route that his heart had marked out. When, for example, Endymion had traveled the " journey homeward to habitual self " and was buried in his own deadly selfhood,[1] he was prepared for deliverance from " this rapacious deep " in three stages. First, the riches of nature appeared before him: " the floral pride / In a long whispering birth enchanted grew / Before his footsteps." [2] Then music: " This still alarm, / This sleepy music, forc'd him walk tiptoe." [3] At length, surrounded by cupids, he observed the love-visitation of Venus and Adonis. And now at last " some ethereal and high-favouring donor " has presented " immortal bowers to mortal sense." [4] By ascending the ladder of intensities, Endymion, too, has been released from the prison house of his mortal self and has attained insight into the mortal-immortal nature of heaven's bourne.

In Keats' ballad these increasing enthrallments of selfhood appear in successive order, each occupying one of three successive stanzas (5, 6, 7); and they lead finally to the heaven's bourne of the elfin grot (8). In folk literature the interiors of hills are often the dwelling places of fairies and elves: Tam Lin dwelled in a green hill, and in the romance of " Thomas of Erceldoune," which deals with the same Thomas Rymer, the hero was led " in at Eldone hill." Apparently the tradition of elfin grots was especially appropriate to Keats' purpose. Earthly in its form and yet " elfin " in its nature—within the cold hill side of the physical world and yet being the otherworld mystery within the physical—it corresponds to the oxymoronic realm where life's self is nourished by its proper pith and to which man can ascend by a ladder of intensities. It is the earth spiritually transfigured; its fairyhood is the " leaven, /

---

[1] *Endymion,* II. 276.
[2] *Ibid.,* 345-47.
[3] *Ibid.,* 357-58.
[4] *Ibid.,* 437-38.

That spreading in this dull and clodded earth / Gives it a touch ethereal."

In calling upon another analogue to Keats' ballad I do not mean to propose that Keats was directly influenced by it, despite the possibility that he was. Even proof of Keats' indebtedness, could it be found, would be irrelevant to our purpose, for it could not charge his ballad with values not already inherent in it. Nevertheless, it is illuminating to observe what significances the legend of Thomas Rymer held forth to one of Keats' contemporaries, an intimate friend of John Hamilton Reynolds and therefore one who was undoubtedly known to Keats. In the summer of 1818, nearly a year before Keats composed " La Belle Dame Sans Merci," John F. M. Dovaston wrote his " Elfin Bride, a Fairy Ballad," although it seems not to have appeared in print until 1825.[5] Its source is not the folk ballad but the mediaeval romance " Thomas of Erceldoune," which is a more extended version of the same legend.

The argument of the " Elfin Bride," Dovaston wrote, is that " Time has no existence but with motion and matter: with the Deity, ' whose centre is everywhere, and circumference nowhere,'— and with ' millions of spiritual creatures ' . . . Duration is without Time." Apparently the legend of Thomas has the power of provoking speculations about a condition in which love is forever warm and still to be enjoyed. In Dovaston's ballad Merlin is substituted for Thomas Rymer, his fellow in many mediaeval legends. Merlin meets a " White Lady " and begs of her that he may see " that airy country / That wots not of Time nor Place." They ride away on palfreys to fairyland, where Merlin is treated to a multitude of " pleasures refin'd." The passing time seems only a moment, but Merlin is informed that " to Man in the dull cold world thou hast left, / Seven times four Seasons are gone." When, however, Merlin attempts a physical consummation of his love, the ideal

[5] *Poems, Legendary, Incidental, and Humorous,* Shrewsbury, 1825.

[71]

vision is shattered, and he finds himself once again in the world of time and place, which now seems to him insipid and decayed although the memory of the fairy music still rings in his ear:

> *He gazed all around the dull heathy ground,*
> *Neither tree nor bush was there,*
> *But wide wide wide all on every side*
> *Spread the heath dry brown and bare.*

Returning once again to fairyland, Merlin remains for seven more years until at last a longing grows in him for the mortal and mutable world: he thought

> *on the vales and green mountains of Wales*
> *And his friends so long forgot.*

> *For blithe are the vales and green mountains of Wales*
> *And its blithe to sojourn there.*

The wish is sufficient to free him from the land without time and place.

> *Then suddenly there small shrilly and clear*
> *The Fairy-folk ceas'd their singing,*
> *And the silvery swells of pipes and bells*
> *No longer around him were ringing.*

> *And the Fairyland gay all melted away*
> *In a misty vapour curl'd;*
> *And his opening eyes beheld with surprize*
> *The light of this long-left world.*

Driven back to earth by his human desires, Merlin awakens to find that his life in fairyland has been a vision, that but a moment has passed, and that he is still in the summer bower where he was when his dream began. Although Dovaston, unlike Keats, drew from his narrative the conclusion that man should be content with his mortal lot, it is obvious that he also found in the legend of Thomas Rymer a myth of a spaceless, timeless realm of pleasure from which man withdraws when the mortal world beckons him and from which he is cast out when he attempts to realize physically the ideal pleasures. In all this one cannot avoid hearing echoes of the "Ode on a Grecian Urn."

With Dovaston's ballad in mind we can see even more clearly the meaningfulness of the narrative pattern into which Keats wove the increasing intensities that mark the journey to the elfin grot. Now, dreams often perform in Keats' system of thought the function of the imagination. It is, for example, in dream visions that Endymion is united with Cynthia and hence gains insight into the beauty-truth of heaven's bourne. "The Imagination," Keats wrote, "may be compared to Adam's dream—he awoke and found it truth." [6] "Real are the dreams of Gods," [7] for to them beauty is truth, not merely a foreshadowing of it, as the visions of the human imagination are; but for the man who lives a life of sensations, dreams may at least be prefigurative visions of the beauty-truth reality to come. Therefore, ideally, having ascended the pleasure thermometer, the knight should perceive an immortality of passion, especially since his vision-making imagination is aided by fairy magic.

But the tug of the mutable world is too strong for mere mortals because "in the world / We jostle" [8] and, as Dovaston wrote, we are drawn away by thoughts of "the vales and green mountains of Wales / And . . . friends so long forgot." Even in the heart of his prefigurative visions of heaven's bourne earthly man recalls that human passions leave a heart high-sorrowful and cloyed; his spirit clings to the vision until "the stings / Of human neighbourhood envenom all." [9] Merlin found that the desire to consummate physically his love for the "White Lady" cast him upon "the heath dry brown and bare," the cold hill side from which one sees

[6] Letter to Bailey, November 22, 1817.
[7] "Lamia," I. 127.
[8] "To J. H. Reynolds, Esq.," 71-72.   [9] *Endymion,* I. 621-22.

only withered sedge and hears no song of birds. And yet, this is a
fate that must befall all mortal aspirations, for so long as man is
earth-bound his life is made up of

> the war, the deeds,
> The disappointment, the anxiety,
> Imagination's struggles, far and nigh,
> All human.[10]

Mortal life must necessarily be an incessant struggle against
these ills, which are ineradicable; living is the very act of being
militant against the dimensional restrictions of the world. And
thus all mortals who engage in " Imagination's struggles " are
knights-at-arms. But man cannot gain his quest in this world.
No knight-at-arms can remain in the elfin grot because, since he is
mortal, he cannot wholly yield himself up to this extra-human realm
and gain visionary insight into its nature. He will be impelled to
make the visionary physical or will long for " his friends so long
forgot." This is precisely the realization that came to Keats when
he wrote of his visit to Burns' country:

> Scanty the hour and few the steps beyond the bourn of care,
> Beyond the sweet and bitter world,—beyond it unaware!
> Scanty the hour and few the steps, because a longer stay
> Would bar return, and make a man forget his mortal way:
> O horrible! to lose the sight of well remember'd face,
> Of Brother's eyes, of Sister's brow. . . .
> No, no, that horror cannot be, for at the cable's length
> Man feels the gentle anchor pull and gladdens in its strength.[11]

It is man's bond with mankind that prevents him from lingering
beyond the bourne of care. There is nothing in Keats' ballad even
suggesting the frequent interpretation that the fairy's child is

---

[10] *Ibid.*, II. 153-56.
[11] " Lines Written in the Highlands after a Visit to Burns's Country," 29-40.

responsible for the knight's expulsion from the elfin grot; only his own inherent attribute of being mortal causes his magic withdrawal, as only the call of Merlin's human and physical impulses caused "the Fairyland gay" to melt in a misty vapor. The vision of the mortal-immortal can only entice mortal man towards heaven's bourne; it cannot aid him in his aspirations or preserve his vision, which must inevitably be shattered. By this fair enchantment mortal man can only be "tortured with renewed life." [12]

It is in this sense that la belle dame is sans merci, without tenderness; this is a description of what provokes man's aspirations, rather than an evaluation of it. Like the lady of the tradition of courtly love, she is the ideal whom the lover must pursue but whom he can never possess; and hence he is doomed to suffer her "unkindness," which is her nature although not her fault. Only the inherent meanness of man's dreams, then, draws him back from heaven's bourne, for, instead of being visionary penetrations into that final essence which is beauty-truth, they are only of mutable things. Aspire though he will, the stings of human neighborhood envenom all.

Instead of dreaming of the "ardent listlessness" which is heaven, the knight finds that death-pale kings, princes, and warriors intrude into his dream, mortal man being the necessary symbol of transitoriness and decay. What man calls living is truly the act of dying, since it is an incessant progress towards the grave; it is what Pope described as "that long disease, my life." Only after death, when man can exist in heaven's bourne, does he truly live; and therefore all earthly men are death-pale. Being mortal, and therefore death-pale, is also the condition of being cut off from that realm of pure being where life's self is nourished by its own pith. As death-pale man lives his existence of decay he can only yearn for that region from which his spirit comes, from which it has been

[12] *Endymion*, I. 919.

divorced, but in which is the vital principle which will hereafter feed his spirit with " renewed life." Thus the lips of all mortal men are starved for lack of their spirit's own pith, for lack of the germ of spirit that is to be sucked from " mould ethereal." [13]

Yet, instead of aspiring to this spiritual food of heaven, as the knight does, mortal man has circumscribed himself by the physical world, and though death-pale and spiritually starved, fears the attraction of heaven's bourne. The impulse in that direction, Keats wrote in *Endymion*, leaves one " too happy to be glad," " More happy than betides mortality." [14] " It is a flaw / In happiness to see beyond our bourn." [15] Therefore, fearful of the aspiration that agonizes and spoils the apparent splendor of the material world, mortality, despite its own sufferings, warns the knight that " La Belle Dame sans Merci / Hath thee in thrall! " How strange it is, Keats once mused,

> *that man on earth should roam,*
> *And lead a life of woe, but not forsake*
> *His rugged path; nor dare he view alone*
> *His future doom which is but to awake.*[16]

It is significant that the warning comes from those who seek to battle the world's ills (warriors) and from men of power (kings and princes). " I would call the top and head of those who have a proper self," Keats wrote, " Men of Power "; [17] that is, men who cannot ascend the pleasure thermometer and lose their selves in essence because they are self-contained.

The knight's inherent weakness in being unable to exclude from his visions the self-contained and world-bound mortality dissipates

[13] Letter to Reynolds, February 19, 1818.
[14] *Endymion*, IV. 819, 859.
[15] " To J. H. Reynolds, Esq.," 82-83.
[16] " On Death."
[17] Letter to Bailey, November 22, 1817.

the ideal into which he has entered momentarily, just as the need for the world of men and the desire to materialize the ideal destroy the fairyland for Merlin. The elfin grot once again becomes the cold hill side which is the physical, mutable world, where the knight has been all the while, but which, by means of his visionary insight, took on the magic splendor of the elfin grot, the mystery within the mutable. The vision had momentarily transfigured a real thing into an " ethereal " thing. Exactly so, it was the poet's vision that transformed the marble embroidery on the Grecian urn into the unchanging vitality of a realm without space, time, and identity; and the shattering of that vision once again froze the immortality of passion into cold, motionless marble. With the dissipation of the vision in the ballad and with the consequent return to the cold physical world, the ladder of intensities which the knight had ascended to reach the ethereal world now crumbles beneath him: love has gone, " the sedge has wither'd from the lake," and " no birds sing." Love, song, and nature fade and disappear as the knight's capacity for the passionate intensity for fellowship with essence becomes enervate and he returns to normal human weakness.

Now that the knight has been awakened from his dream by the stings of human neighborhood, he is as pale, death-pale, as the kings, princes, and warriors, for he now shares their mortality. Being mortal, his very existence is a progress towards death, and death therefore is in his nature, although in the elfin grot existence, being without time, is without death. Indeed, Keats originally wrote, " I see *death's* lilly on thy brow . . . And on thy cheeks *death's* fading rose." By withdrawing from the elfin grot, the knight has also become a Man of Power; the withdrawal is the act of reassuming his own self-containing identity, and thus he is " alone," being his own isolated self. His aloneness is the opposite of a fellowship with essence which absorbs the proper self, that self which is cut off from its selfless origin in heaven. At heaven's bourne there can be no aloneness because there are no individual selves, no proper identities; there it is irrelevant to ask, " Who are these coming to the sacrifice? " Earthly life, then, is a spiritual solitude overcast with the pallor of death, and a denial of the " honey wild, and manna dew," the heaven-sent food which is life's proper pith; all mortal living is a movement towards the sacrificial altar. " Living," therefore, must be a biding of one's time, a meaningless exhausting of one's mortal lease, since man is only a temporary resident in this world. The elfin grot being truly his home ethereal, mortal man, in the solitude of his self, can only " sojourn here, . . . palely loitering " on the cold hill side of the world. And the unfinished, hovering quality of the metrics of each stanzaic close (" And no birds sing," " On the cold hill's side ") perfectly reinforces the aimless solitude with which Keats is investing mortal life.

iii

We have already noticed the organization of the poem into two discourses—the questions of the stranger in the first three stanzas, and the knight's reply in the following nine. But within this pattern, another, more intricate and significant, is at work. In this inner configuration the poem falls into four equal groups of three stanzas each, the first of which is the symbol-making address of the stranger. The next six stanzas, the narrative core of the poem, tell of the direct relations of the knight and the fairy lady; of these the first three constitute one unit, and the last three another, the grouping and distinctness being marked by the two opening patterns: " I met," " I made," " I set "; and " She found," " She took," " And there she lulled me." The final unit of three stanzas in the poem is a kind of epilogue telling of the aftermath of the encounter with the fairy's child and thus answers the stranger's questions in the three introductory stanzas and brings the poem round full circle so that the final stanza may be an approximate repetition of the first. This last unit is also bound together, nearly as the second three stanzas are: " I saw," " I saw," " And this is why I sojourn here."

But with these balances and intricacies Keats is not merely carving his narrative into fascinating arabesques. His artistry is almost always functional to his meaning and is seldom an end in itself. In stanza four it is noticeable that the only actor is the knight. In the next stanza the knight controls the action of the first two lines, and the lady that of the second two. In stanza six he truly governs only the first line, and it seems significant that Keats altered the action of the folk ballad, where it is the lady who takes Thomas upon her horse. Apparently there is a special intent in giving the action to the knight in the first line so that he may remain an actor throughout these three stanzas, but with diminishing control over the action. Clearly the lady governs the action in the last two lines of stanza six and, in a broader sense, the action of the second line also, for the stanza states that the knight's seeing nothing else is the consequence of the lady's singing.

There is, then, a progressive shrinkage of the " I " as a power and a corresponding dominance of the " she," until in stanza seven, where the height of the pleasure thermometer is reached, the lady alone controls the entire action, and the knight passively yields to her. The consequence of ascending the pleasure thermometer, it will be recalled, is that one enters into the essences of progressive intensities, which are " Richer entanglements, enthralments far / More self-destroying." And proportionately as the knight ascends from nature to song to love, his active self is being absorbed into the ideal, which increasingly exercises control over his self. It is in this sense of empathic enthrallment that the knight is cautioned, " La Belle Dame sans Merci / Hath thee in *thrall!* " Once he has wilfully entered into sensuous essence and set up the lady as an ideal (" I set her on my pacing steed "), he has abandoned his selfhood; even the apparently wilfull act of looking at the fairy's child is the passive consequence of being so absorbed into the essence of song that he can perceive only ideality: " And nothing else saw all day long." Since those who have " a proper self " are " Men of Power," the retreat of the " I " and the emergence of the " she " as the sources of activity are the grammatical dramatization of the destruction of that power as the knight enters into greater and greater enthrallments.

At the tip-top of the humanly attainable scale is the " orbed drop / Of light, and that is love "; " Nor with aught else can our souls interknit / So wingedly." Consequently, in stanza seven, in which the lady expresses her love, she is the only power, and the knight is completely enthralled by essence, ready now to enter into the heaven's bourne of the elfin grot. Moreover, the interknitting of the soul with essence through love so elevates the soul that it may partake of the spiritual stuff of which it is itself made, and hence " Life's self is nourish'd by its proper pith, / And we are nurtured like a pelican brood." In other words, by the knight's entrance into essence through love the ideal nourishes him with the source of his own spiritual mystery—with " roots of relish sweet, / And honey wild, and manna dew."

The structural pattern of the main narrative stanzas (4–12) is, then, as precisely balanced as that of the " Ode on a Grecian Urn." In the ode the first two stanzas trace the ascent to a perception of the frieze as a timeless, spaceless, selfless realm of endless vitality; the last two, the descent from this realm, bring the poem back to the condition from which it started. And the central stanza both depicts the oxymoronic nature of this area and introduces the chemicals for its destruction. Correspondingly, the first four stanzas (4–7) of the main narrative in the ballad lead towards the oxymoronic elfin grot; the last four (9–12), away from it. And the central stanza (8) both admits the knight into the elfin grot and motivates the dissolution of the vision, for in this stanza the knight takes it upon himself to shut the " wild wild eyes " of the mystery. In the ode, the heaven's bourne of the frieze is dispelled by a force within the poet himself, the unavoidable recollection of the mortal world; in the ballad, a force within the mortal knight—not an act of the fairy's child—causes him to shut out the wild mystery of the ideal. The tug of mortality converts the timeless and spaceless, but vital, frieze into a physical activity in the ever-recurring journey from the town-world to the altar-heaven; the tug of mortality converts the inward mystery of the elfin grot into its outward and merely physical form, the cold hill side.

With the dissolution of heaven's bourne and of the knight's complete assimilation into essence in stanza seven, the grammatical controls in the poem retrieve his selfhood until once again he is wholly self-contained. The " stings of human neighbourhood " have envenomed all; and thus when " thoughts of self came on," he travels " The journey homeward to habitual self." Therefore the empathic order of stanzas four to seven is inverted. In stanza eight the lady governs the action of the first two lines, and the knight that of the last two, for it is the interfering power of his own mortal identity that shuts out the mystery. In the next stanza the lady controls only the action of the first line, and the knight that of the last three. And now at last the knight has fully emerged from the enthrallment, and his self is dominant in the remaining three stanzas. The empathic involvement and withdrawal that were enacted in the " Ode on a Grecian Urn " by dramatic gesture and verbal moods are here enacted by overt dramatic action and by the gradual transfer of grammatical control from one actor to the other.

One of the remarkable features of the ballad is the intricate interlacing of the meaningfully balanced patterns we have been examining. In one sense the first three stanzas are introductory to the following narrative. Within this main narrative (4–12) the action is perfectly pivoted on the central stanza (8), the narrative, the symbols, and the grammatical controls symmetrically rising to and falling away from this central point. And in yet another sense, the first three stanzas (1–3) and the last three (10–12) are prologue and epilogue, the central six (4–9) being perfectly balanced by the distribution of the opening patterns, " I " and " she." Since we have seen a similar meaningful balance in the " Ode on a Grecian Urn," we might well suspect that Keats is far from being merely an associative poet whose only control over structure is the subjective pattern that his feelings spontaneously dictated to him. Quite to the contrary, Keats conceived of a poem as a perfectly ordered cosmos, an experience not only completed but also self-contained by reason of its circularity. And this perfect circularity— because of which he delighted in what he called the " rondeau "— not only is a control over the work of art as a poetic microcosm but also is itself a meaning functional to the poem. That this sense of the complete and organically meaningful architecture of a work of art was deep in Keats' poetic conceptions is clear from the second of his three axioms of poetry. The touches of beauty in poetry, he wrote,

> should never be half way thereby making the reader breathless instead of content: the rise, the progress, the setting of imagery should like the Sun come natural to him—shine over him and set soberly although in magnificence leaving him in the Luxury of twilight.[18]

iv

What emerges from this analysis is that " La Belle Dame Sans Merci " has grown out of the same body of conceptions, beliefs, and aspirations that motivate the " Ode on a Grecian Urn," and that it is shaped by the same mode of poetic perception. The major

---

[18] Letter to Taylor, February 27, 1818.

difference between the ode and the ballad is that the latter fails to attain the high consolation of the last stanza of the ode; but otherwise the ballad is the projection into myth of what was experienced in the ode as symbol. The increase in psychic distance gained by translating the drama within the consciousness of the poet into objective correlatives allows the poet to stretch out into the chronological span of a narrative a drama that he could express in the ode only as the evolving inward recognition of symbolic values. But the same sense of great harmonic control appears in both poems in their meaningfully pivoted structure and in the interweaving of patterns. And both are variant artistic intertextures of the three coexistent themes that dominate Keats' deepest meditations and profoundest system of values: the oxymoronic heaven's bourne towards which his spirit yearned; the pleasure thermometer which he conceived of as the spiritual path to that goal; and the self-annihilation that he understood to be the condition necessary for the journey. In this sense the ballad differs from the ode essentially in enacting this triune drama in a realm of space and time; and hence the self-conscious identity of the poet becomes the knight, the coexistent symbols of the thermometer are spread out into a context of time, and the journey heavenward is a passage through a spatial world.

Yet, because the ballad lacks the resolution of the ode, the differences are immense. In his discovery that art prefigures an attainable heaven where beauty will be truth, Keats spoke to man an Everlasting Yea; "La Belle Dame Sans Merci" is his Center of Indifference.

The Eve of St. Agnes

I

St. Agnes' Eve—Ah, bitter chill it was!
The owl, for all his feathers, was a-cold;
The hare limp'd trembling through the frozen grass,
And silent was the flock in woolly fold:
Numb were the Beadsman's fingers, while he told
His rosary, and while his frosted breath,
Like pious incense from a censer old,
Seem'd taking flight for heaven, without a death,
Past the sweet Virgin's picture, while his prayer he saith.

II

His prayer he saith, this patient, holy man;   10
Then takes his lamp, and riseth from his knees,
And back returneth, meagre, barefoot, wan,
Along the chapel aisle by slow degrees:
The sculptur'd dead, on each side, seem to freeze,
Emprison'd in black, purgatorial rails:
Knights, ladies, praying in dumb orat'ries,
He passeth by; and his weak spirit fails
To think how they may ache in icy hoods and mails.

III

Northward he turneth through a little door,
And scarce three steps, ere Music's golden tongue   20
Flatter'd to tears this aged man and poor;
But no—already had his deathbell rung;
The joys of all his life were said and sung:
His was harsh penance on St. Agnes' Eve:
Another way he went, and soon among
Rough ashes sat he for his soul's reprieve,
And all night kept awake, for sinners' sake to grieve.

IV

That ancient Beadsman heard the prelude soft;
And so it chanc'd, for many a door was wide,
From hurry to and fro. Soon, up aloft,   30
The silver, snarling trumpets 'gan to chide:
The level chambers, ready with their pride,
Were glowing to receive a thousand guests:
The carved angels, ever eager-eyed,
Star'd, where upon their heads the cornice rests,
With hair blown back, and wings put cross-wise on their breasts.

V

At length burst in the argent revelry,
With plume, tiara, and all rich array,
Numerous as shadows haunting fairily
The brain, new stuff'd, in youth, with triumphs gay   40
Of old romance. These let us wish away,
And turn, sole-thoughted, to one Lady there,
Whose heart had brooded, all that wintry day,
On love, and wing'd St. Agnes' saintly care,
As she had heard old dames full many times declare.

VI

They told her how, upon St. Agnes' Eve,
Young virgins might have visions of delight,
And soft adorings from their loves receive
Upon the honey'd middle of the night,
If ceremonies due they did aright;   50
As, supperless to bed they must retire,
And couch supine their beauties, lily white;
Nor look behind, nor sideways, but require
Of Heaven with upward eyes for all that they desire.

VII

Full of this whim was thoughtful Madeline:
The music, yearning like a God in pain,

She scarcely heard: her maiden eyes divine,
Fix'd on the floor, saw many a sweeping train
Pass by—she heeded not at all: in vain
Came many a tiptoe, amorous cavalier,   60
And back retir'd; not cool'd by high disdain,
But she saw not: her heart was otherwhere:
She sigh'd for Agnes' dreams, the sweetest of the year.

VIII

She danc'd along with vague, regardless eyes,
Anxious her lips, her breathing quick and short:
The hallow'd hour was near at hand: she sighs
Amid the timbrels, and the throng'd resort
Of whisperers in anger, or in sport;
'Mid looks of love, defiance, hate, and scorn,
Hoodwink'd with faery fancy; all amort,   70
Save to St. Agnes and her lambs unshorn,
And all the bliss to be before to-morrow morn.

IX

So, purposing each moment to retire,
She linger'd still. Meantime, across the moors,
Had come young Porphyro, with heart on fire
For Madeline. Beside the portal doors,
Buttress'd from moonlight, stands he, and implores
All saints to give him sight of Madeline,
But for one moment in the tedious hours,
That he might gaze and worship all unseen;   80
Perchance speak, kneel, touch, kiss—in sooth such things
                                have been.

X

He ventures in: let no buzz'd whisper tell:
All eyes be muffled, or a hundred swords
Will storm his heart, Love's fev'rous citadel:
For him, those chambers held barbarian hordes,
Hyena foemen, and hot-blooded lords,

Whose very dogs would execrations howl
Against his lineage: not one breast affords
Him any mercy, in that mansion foul,
Save one old beldame, weak in body and in soul.   90

XI

Ah, happy chance! the aged creature came,
Shuffling along with ivory-headed wand,
To where he stood, hid from the torch's flame,
Behind a broad hall-pillar, far beyond
The sound of merriment and chorus bland:
He startled her; but soon she knew his face,
And grasp'd his fingers in her palsied hand,
Saying, ' Mercy, Porphyro! hie thee from this place;
' They are all here to-night, the whole blood-thirsty race!

XII

' Get hence! get hence! there's dwarfish Hildebrand;   100
' He had a fever late, and in the fit
' He cursed thee and thine, both house and land:
' Then there's that old Lord Maurice, not a whit
' More tame for his gray hairs—Alas me! flit!
' Flit like a ghost away.'—'Ah, Gossip dear,
' We're safe enough; here in this arm-chair sit,
' And tell me how '—' Good Saints! not here, not here;
' Follow me, child, or else these stones will be thy bier.'

XIII

He follow'd through a lowly arched way,
Brushing the cobwebs with his lofty plume,   110
And as she mutter'd ' Well-a—well-a-day!'
He found him in a little moonlight room,
Pale, lattic'd, chill, and silent as a tomb.
' Now tell me where is Madeline,' said he,
' O tell me, Angela, by the holy loom
' Which none but secret sisterhood may see,
' When they St. Agnes' wool are weaving piously.'

XIV

'St. Agnes! Ah! it is St. Agnes' Eve—
'Yet men will murder upon holy days:
'Thou must hold water in a witch's sieve,   120
'And be liege-lord of all the Elves and Fays,
'To venture so: it fills me with amaze
'To see thee, Porphyro!—St. Agnes' Eve!
'God's help! my lady fair the conjuror plays
'This very night: good angels her deceive!
'But let me laugh awhile, I've mickle time to grieve.'

XV

Feebly she laugheth in the languid moon,
While Porphyro upon her face doth look,
Like puzzled urchin on an aged crone
Who keepeth clos'd a wond'rous riddle-book,   130
As spectacled she sits in chimney nook.
But soon his eyes grew brilliant, when she told
His lady's purpose; and he scarce could brook
Tears, at the thought of those enchantments cold
And Madeline asleep in lap of legends old.

XVI

Sudden a thought came like a full-blown rose,
Flushing his brow, and in his pained heart
Made purple riot: then doth he propose
A stratagem, that makes the beldame start: .
'A cruel man and impious thou art: 140
'Sweet lady, let her pray, and sleep, and dream
'Alone with her good angels, far apart
'From wicked men like thee. Go, go!—I deem
'Thou canst not surely be the same that thou didst seem.'

XVII

'I will not harm her, by all saints I swear,'
Quoth Porphyro: 'O may I ne'er find grace

'When my weak voice shall whisper its last prayer,
'If one of her soft ringlets I displace,
'Or look with ruffian passion in her face:
'Good Angela, believe me by these tears;   150
'Or I will, even in a moment's space,
'Awake, with horrid shout, my foemen's ears,
'And beard them, though they be more fang'd than wolves
                                                  and bears.'

XVIII

'Ah! why wilt thou affright a feeble soul?
'A poor, weak, palsy-stricken, churchyard thing,
'Whose passing-bell may ere the midnight toll;
'Whose prayers for thee, each morn and evening,
'Were never miss'd.'—Thus plaining, doth she bring
A gentler speech from burning Porphyro;
So woful, and of such deep sorrowing,   160
That Angela gives promise she will do
Whatever he shall wish, betide her weal or woe.

XIX

Which was, to lead him, in close secrecy,
Even to Madeline's chamber, and there hide
Him in a closet, of such privacy
That he might see her beauty unespied,
And win perhaps that night a peerless bride,
While legion'd fairies pac'd the coverlet,
And pale enchantment held her sleepy-eyed.
Never on such a night have lovers met,   170
Since Merlin paid his Demon all the monstrous debt.

XX

'It shall be as thou wishest,' said the Dame:
'All cates and dainties shall be stored there
'Quickly on this feast-night: by the tambour frame
'Her own lute thou wilt see: no time to spare,
'For I am slow and feeble, and scarce dare

'On such a catering trust my dizzy head.
'Wait here, my child, with patience; kneel in prayer
'The while: Ah! thou must needs the lady wed,
'Or may I never leave my grave among the dead.'   180

XXI

So saying, she hobbled off with busy fear.
The lover's endless minutes slowly pass'd;
The dame return'd, and whisper'd in his ear
To follow her; with aged eyes aghast
From fright of dim espial. Safe at last,
Through many a dusky gallery, they gain
The maiden's chamber, silken, hush'd, and chaste;
Where Porphyro took covert, pleas'd amain.
His poor guide hurried back with agues in her brain.

XXII

Her falt'ring hand upon the balustrade,   190
Old Angela was feeling for the stair,
When Madeline, St. Agnes' charmed maid,
Rose, like a mission'd spirit, unaware:
With silver taper's light, and pious care,
She turn'd, and down the aged gossip led
To a safe level matting. Now prepare,
Young Porphyro, for gazing on that bed;
She comes, she comes again, like ring-dove fray'd and fled.

XXIII

Out went the taper as she hurried in;
Its little smoke, in pallid moonshine, died: 200
She clos'd the door, she panted, all akin
To spirits of the air, and visions wide:
No uttered syllable, or, woe betide!
But to her heart, her heart was voluble,
Paining with eloquence her balmy side;
As though a tongueless nightingale should swell
Her throat in vain, and die, heart-stifled, in her dell.

[90]

XXIV

A casement high and triple-arch'd there was,
All garlanded with carven imag'ries
Of fruits, and flowers, and bunches of knot-grass,   210
And diamonded with panes of quaint device,
Innumerable of stains and splendid dyes,
As are the tiger-moth's deep-damask'd wings;
And in the midst, 'mong thousand heraldries,
And twilight saints, and dim emblazonings,
A shielded scutcheon blush'd with blood of queens and kings.

XXV

Full on this casement shone the wintry moon,
And threw warm gules on Madeline's fair breast,
As down she knelt for heaven's grace and boon;
Rose-bloom fell on her hands, together prest,   220
And on her silver cross soft amethyst,
And on her hair a glory, like a saint:
She seem'd a splendid angel, newly drest,
Save wings, for heaven:—Porphyro grew faint:
She knelt, so pure a thing, so free from mortal taint.

XXVI

Anon his heart revives: her vespers done,
Of all its wreathed pearls her hair she frees;
Unclasps her warmed jewels one by one;
Loosens her fragrant boddice; by degrees
Her rich attire creeps rustling to her knees: 230
Half-hidden, like a mermaid in sea-weed,
Pensive awhile she dreams awake, and sees,
In fancy, fair St. Agnes in her bed,
But dares not look behind, or all the charm is fled.

XXVII

Soon, trembling in her soft and chilly nest,
In sort of wakeful swoon, perplex'd she lay,

Until the poppied warmth of sleep oppress'd
Her soothed limbs, and soul fatigued away;
Flown, like a thought, until the morrow-day;
Blissfully haven'd both from joy and pain;   240
Clasp'd like a missal where swart Paynims pray;
Blinded alike from sunshine and from rain,
As though a rose should shut, and be a bud again.

XXVIII

Stol'n to this paradise, and so entranced,
Porphyro gazed upon her empty dress,
And listen'd to her breathing, if it chanced
To wake into a slumberous tenderness;
Which when he heard, that minute did he bless,
And breath'd himself: then from the closet crept,
Noiseless as fear in a wide wilderness,   250
And over the hush'd carpet, silent, stept,
And 'tween the curtains peep'd, where, lo!—how fast she slept.

XXIX

Then by the bed-side, where the faded moon
Made a dim, silver twilight, soft he set
A table, and, half anguish'd, threw thereon
A cloth of woven crimson, gold, and jet:—
O for some drowsy Morphean amulet!
The boisterous, midnight, festive clarion,
The kettle-drum, and far-heard clarionet,
Affray his ears, though but in dying tone:—   260
The hall door shuts again, and all the noise is gone.

XXX

And still she slept an azure-lidded sleep,
In blanched linen, smooth, and lavender'd,
While he from forth the closet brought a heap
Of candied apple, quince, and plum, and gourd
With jellies soother than the creamy curd,

And lucent syrops, tinct with cinnamon;
Manna and dates, in argosy transferr'd
From Fez; and spiced dainties, every one,
From silken Samarcand to cedar'd Lebanon.   270

XXXI

These delicates he heap'd with glowing hand
On golden dishes and in baskets bright
Of wreathed silver: sumptuous they stand
In the retired quiet of the night,
Filling the chilly room with perfume light.—
'And now, my love, my seraph fair, awake!
'Thou art my heaven, and I thine eremite:
'Open thine eyes, for meek St. Agnes' sake,
'Or I shall drowse beside thee, so my soul doth ache.'

XXXII

Thus whispering, his warm, unnerved arm   280
Sank in her pillow. Shaded was her dream
By the dusk curtains:—'twas a midnight charm
Impossible to melt as iced stream:
The lustrous salvers in the moonlight gleam;
Broad golden fringe upon the carpet lies:
It seem'd he never, never could redeem
From such a stedfast spell his lady's eyes;
So mus'd awhile, entoil'd in woofed phantasies.

XXXIII

Awakening up, he took her hollow lute,—
Tumultuous,—and, in chords that tenderest be,   290
He play'd an ancient ditty, long since mute,
In Provence call'd, 'La belle dame sans mercy:'
Close to her ear touching the melody;—
Wherewith disturb'd, she utter'd a soft moan:
He ceased—she panted quick—and suddenly
Her blue affrayed eyes wide open shone:
Upon his knees he sank, pale as smooth-sculptured stone.

XXXIV

Her eyes were open, but she still beheld,
Now wide awake, the vision of her sleep:
There was a painful change, that nigh expell'd   300
The blisses of her dream so pure and deep
At which fair Madeline began to weep,
And moan forth witless words with many a sigh;
While still her gaze on Porphyro would keep;
Who knelt, with joined hands and piteous eye,
Fearing to move or speak, she look'd so dreamingly.

XXXV

' Ah, Porphyro!' said she, ' but even now
' Thy voice was at sweet tremble in mine ear,
' Made tuneable with every sweetest vow;
' And those sad eyes were spiritual and clear: 310
' How chang'd thou art! how pallid, chill, and drear!
' Give me that voice again, my Porphyro,
' Those looks immortal, those complainings dear!
' Oh leave me not in this eternal woe,
' For if thou diest, my Love, I know not where to go.'

XXXVI

Beyond a mortal man impassion'd far
At these voluptuous accents, he arose,
Ethereal, flush'd, and like a throbbing star
Seen mid the sapphire heaven's deep repose
Into her dream he melted, as the rose   320
Blendeth its odour with the violet,—
Solution sweet: meantime the frost-wind blows
Like Love's alarum pattering the sharp sleet
Against the window-panes; St. Agnes' moon hath set.

XXXVII

'Tis dark: quick pattereth the flaw-blown sleet:
' This is no dream, my bride, my Madeline!'

'Tis dark: the iced gusts still rave and beat:
' No dream, alas! alas! and woe is mine!
' Porphyro will leave me here to fade and pine.—
' Cruel! what traitor could thee hither bring?   330
' I curse not, for my heart is lost in thine
' Though thou forsakest a deceived thing;—
'A dove forlorn and lost with sick unpruned wing.'

XXXVIII

' My Madeline! sweet dreamer! lovely bride!
' Say, may I be for aye thy vassal blest?
' Thy beauty's shield, heart-shap'd and vermeil dyed?
' Ah, silver shrine, here will I take my rest
' After so many hours of toil and quest,
' A famish'd pilgrim,—saved by miracle.
' Though I have found, I will not rob thy nest   340
' Saving of thy sweet self; if thou think'st well
' To trust, fair Madeline, to no rude infidel.'

XXXIX

' Hark! 'tis an elfin-storm from faery land,
' Of haggard seeming, but a boon indeed:
' Arise—arise! the morning is at hand;—
' The bloated wassaillers will never heed:—
' Let us away, my love, with happy speed;
' There are no ears to hear, or eyes to see,—
' Drown'd all in Rhenish and the sleepy mead:
' Awake! arise! my love, and fearless be,   350
' For o'er the southern moors I have a home for thee.'

XL

She hurried at his words, beset with fears,
For there were sleeping dragons all around,
At glaring watch, perhaps, with ready spears—
Down the wide stairs a darkling way they found.—
In all the house was heard no human sound.

A chain-droop'd lamp was flickering by each door;
The arras, rich with horseman, hawk, and hound,
Flutter'd in the besieging wind's uproar;
And the long carpets rose along the gusty floor.   360

XLI

They glide, like phantoms, into the wide hall;
Like phantoms, to the iron porch, they glide;
Where lay the Porter, in uneasy sprawl,
With a huge empty flaggon by his side:
The wakeful bloodhound rose, and shook his hide,
But his sagacious eye an inmate owns:
By one, and one, the bolts full easy slide:—
The chains lie silent on the footworn stones;—
The key turns, and the door upon its hinges groans.

XLII

And they are gone: ay, ages long ago   370
These lovers fled away into the storm.
That night the Baron dreamt of many a woe,
And all his warrior-guests, with shade and form
Of witch, and demon, and large coffin-worm,
Were long be-nightmar'd. Angela the old
Died palsy-twitch'd, with meagre face deform;
The Beadsman, after thousand aves told,
For aye unsought for slept among his ashes cold.

The Eve of St. Agnes

i

*P*ROBABLY few other poets have ever been interpreted in the light
of such disparate critical premises as Keats has been. The most
pervasive tradition has long since established him as a member of
the art-for-art's-sake school, and it still controls much of the commentary on his poetry. This critical assumption can easily be
arrived at by detaching from their context such statements as " O
for a Life of Sensations rather than of Thoughts," " I look upon
fine phrases like a lover," and " If poetry comes not as naturally as
the leaves to a tree, it had better come not at all " and then assuming that they comprehend all of Keats' artistic intentions.

On this basis poems like the " Ode to Autumn " have been
extolled as pure realization; and " La Belle Dame Sans Merci " has
been held up by those who want poetry to be a heightening of
consciousness but to be innocent of ideas. To Swinburne, Keats
was " the most exclusively aesthetic and the most absolutely non-
moral of all serious writers on record." [1] Arthur Symons understood that Keats lacked " intellectual structure " and that poetry
was his " ideal world, the only aspect of spiritual things which he
ever saw or cared to see; and the thought of poetry, apprehended
for its own sake as the only entirely satisfying thing in the world,
imprisoned him as within a fairy ring, alone with his little circle of
green grass and blue sky." [2] Because of this apparently pure
estheticism Keats was the idol of the Pre-Raphaelites, who first
established critical principles for reading his poetry. So narrow an

[1] *Complete Works* (London, 1925-27), XIV. 158.
[2] *The Romantic Movement in English Poetry* (New York, 1909),
312.

interpretation pictured Keats as only the agent of his own imagination, which was concerned exclusively with the sensuous riches it
might fashion out of the physical things of the world; and it led
Symons, for example, to conclude that even the odes are

> mental picture added to mental picture, separate stanza added
> to separate stanza, rather than the development of a thought
> which must express itself, creating its own form. Meditation
> brings to him no inner vision, no rapture of the soul; but
> seems to germinate upon the page in actual flowers and corn
> and fruit.[3]

Even the passing of estheticism did not affect this representation
of Keats, for it was perpetuated by the patrons of thinginess,
Dinglichkeit. Amy Lowell, for example, repudiated all allegorical
interpretations of *Endymion* and wrote that the poet's feet were
planted " firmly on the good round earth " and his eyes were " busy
beholding the beauties of a material universe which includes friendship, love, and all sorts of human intercourse as well as clouds,
trees, sea, flowers, and moonlight." [4] Nor did the Victorian seekers
after " high seriousness " noticeably alter this view. They were inclined to accept it and therefore to rate Keats as an inferior artist.
Poetry, Arnold decided, " interprets in two ways; it interprets by
expressing with magical felicity the physiognomy and movement of
the outer world and it interprets by expressing with inspired conviction, the ideas and laws of the inward world of man's moral and
spiritual nature." Keats, of course, works in the first and lesser of
these two ways, for in him " the faculty of naturalistic interpretation is overpoweringly predominant, the natural magic perfect." [5]

At the other extreme, largely because of a revolt against the
standards of the Pre-Raphaelites, Keats was later read as a poet of
ideas as though he were obsessed by a thesis which masqueraded in

[3] *Ibid.*, 313.
[4] *John Keats* (London, 1924), I. 456.
[5] *Essays in Criticism, First Series* (London, 1921), 112.

his poetry as things and stories. *Endymion* was elaborately alle-gorized by such commentators as Mrs. F. M. Owen, Robert Bridges, and Hugh l'Anson Fausset; it has long been debated whether Apollonius or Lamia is being condemned, as though " Lamia " were only an excuse for an evaluation of sensuous ex-perience and philosophy; and well-meaning theorists, especially since A. C. Bradley's essay on " Keats and ' Philosophy '," have unfolded the potential philosophic implications of the statement that beauty and truth are identical. Only very recently have critics such as Cleanth Brooks and Kenneth Burke, perceiving the dramatic function of the aphorism in the " Ode on a Grecian Urn," intimated the possibility that Keats' sensibilities are unified at least to this extent: his senses, his imagination, his faith, and his intellect tended to act as interdependent faculties. The ode, we can now see, is neither a set of disjointed mental pictures, nor an excursion into philosophy, nor a gown of lyricism beneath which a petticoat of philosophy is allowed to peep; and we now have at least a justifica-tion for speculating on whether Keats' other poems are not an equal integration of an outer and an inner vision.

But despite these shifting critical standards, " The Eve of St. Agnes " has never been freed from the limitations imposed upon it by the Pre-Raphaelites, to whom it was a kind of prototype of the artistic realization that provides a heightening of consciousness, a more exciting experience than life itself. The following is probably a representative midnineteenth-century evaluation of the poem:

> What a gorgeous gallery of poetic pictures that " Eve of St. Agnes " forms, and yet how slim the tissue that lies below! How thin the canvas on which the whole is painted! For vigorous sense, one deep-thoughted couplet of Dryden would make the whole kick the beam. And yet what can be more exquisite in their way than those pictures of the young poet! [6]

---

[6] Hugh Miller, *Essays* (London, 1856-62), I. 452.

" ' Load every rift ' of your subject with ore," Keats wrote to Shelley; [7] and it has been assumed that " The Eve of St. Agnes " fulfills this doctrine by the density of its riches—its dark and yet gorgeous atmosphere of mediaevalism; the undeviating and spirited directness of its slim narrative; the plump synaesthetic and empathic imagery; the delicate enwrapping of warmth in chill, of quiet in revelry, of love in hate, of youth in age.

To re-examine these effects and the means whereby they are attained would now be a work of supererogation, for the readings of the poem have inevitably been colored by the Victorian discovery that it is a storehouse of narrative, descriptive, atmospheric, and prosodic techniques for building a poetic dream-world. Indeed, the number of such commentaries seems to indicate that Keats succeeded too well in those matters that belong to artistry. Even Fausset, whose study attempts to trace the evolution of Keats' philosophic mind, claims that the romance has " no other aim but the creation of sensuous beauty," and that if Keats' career had ended with the writing of this poem " there would have been every excuse for posterity's acceptance of him as a poet who sought beauty for beauty's sake rather than for truth's." [8] Apparently the corruscating ore packed into the rifts dazzles our attention until we are made careless of the fact that the subject of the poem is the " vast idea " which Keats said ever rolled before his vision. [9]

For it must be clear by now that Keats' most splendid imaginative experiences were one with his most profound conceptions and beliefs. What his imagination seized as beauty was, to him, the truth that is to come; and his poetry most often explores the relation of what we experience as beauty to what we intuit as truth. In this very fact lies the possibility for the ambivalent in-

[7] August 16, 1820.
[8] *Keats, a Study in Development* (London, 1922), 70, 75.
[9] " Sleep and Poetry," 291.

terpretations of his poetry as now sensuous, and now philosophic. Since sensuous experience is prefigurative of ultimate values in Keats' scheme of things, one may wrench out of their context the descriptive splendors and read either the philosophic meanings or the " gorgeous gallery of poetic pictures." But if we accept Keats' own premises concerning the relation of esthetic experience to metaphysical values, we are justified in adopting, at least as a working hypothesis, a belief that a high seriousness, an inner vision, inheres as much in " The Eve of St. Agnes " as it does in " La Belle Dame Sans Merci."

ii

It is most convenient to examine first the central episode of the romance, the union of Madeline and Porphyro, and then to analyse the larger surrounding units until the entire poem is encompassed. The justification for proceeding in this manner is the fact that the structure of the poem is a series of concentric circles that expand and deepen each other's meaning.

The most striking feature about the climax is the peculiar confusion of wake and sleep that characterizes Madeline's perception of Porphyro when she is being roused from her vision:

> *Her eyes were open, but she still beheld,*
> *Now wide awake, the vision of her sleep.* (298-299)

We have already seen that in Keats' mind dreams are synonymous with imagination, for both are powers whereby man may penetrate into heaven's bourne, where the intensities of mortal life are repeated in a finer tone and divested of their mutability. Keats had linked sleep and poetry in the title of one of his early poems and there asked " what is higher beyond thought " than sleep. What, that is, brings us closer to heaven's bourne? Sleep comes

> *sometimes like a gentle whispering*
> *Of all the secrets of some wond'rous thing*

[101]

That breathes about us in the vacant air;
So that we look around with prying stare,
Perhaps to see shapes of light, aerial lymning,
And catch soft floatings from a faint-heard hymning;
To see the laurel wreath, on high suspended,
That is to crown our name when life is ended.
Sometimes it gives a glory to the voice,
And from the heart up-springs " Rejoice! rejoice! "
Sounds which will reach the Framer of all things,
And die away in ardent mutterings.[10]

Moreover, Madeline's dream does not take place in the ordinary course of mortal events but is occasioned by the mystical power of St. Agnes' Eve, when, by observing special rites, " Young virgins might have visions of delight " (47). It is a " hallow'd hour " (66), an extraordinary condition that, being outside the normal framework of experience, permits the imagination to rise to super-natural heights and correspondingly to penetrate most deeply into the beauty-truth that is to come. If dreams are imaginative visions of a future reality, St. Agnes' dreams are " the sweetest of the year " (63).

The relation of dream-visions to the imagination, and the manner in which they both function, were most clearly stated by Keats in a famous letter to Bailey.[11] " I am certain of nothing," he wrote,

> but of the holiness of the Heart's affections and the truth of Imagination—What the imagination seizes as Beauty must be truth—whether it existed before or not. . . . The Imagina-tion may be compared to Adam's dream—he awoke and found it truth.

The reference is to that passage in *Paradise Lost* in which Adam tells of the creation of Eve. Overcome as with " an object that

---

[10] *Ibid.*, 29-40.   [11] November 22, 1817.

excels the sense," " Dazzl'd and spent " by the power of God's
" Colloquy sublime," Adam fell into a sleep:

> *Mine eyes he clos'd, but op'n left the Cell*
> *Of Fancy my internal sight, by which*
> *Abstract as in a trance methought I saw,*
> *Though sleeping. . . .*

In this divine trance Adam saw the creation of Eve,

> *so lovely fair,*
> *That what seem'd fair in all the World, seem'd now*
> *Mean, or in her summ'd up.*

Awakening, he found his dream to be true, for before him was the
corporeal beauty,

> *Such as I saw her in my dream, adorn'd*
> *With what all Earth or Heaven could bestow*
> *To make her amiable.*[12]

God had fulfilled his pledge to Adam to realize " Thy wish, exactly
to thy heart's desire." Now, by making of Adam's dream in Eden
a parable of the imagination Keats certainly did not mean that we
shall know in our mortal careers that our imaginings are true; here
we can know only a beauty that must die, but in awakening into
the reality to come we shall discover that the extraordinary imaginative insights we experience here will hereafter be experienced
under the conditions of immortality. Our earthly visions of an Eve,
who is our heart's desire, the essence of all the beauty that earth or
heaven can bestow or our imaginations fashion, will hereafter be
enjoyed as immutable realities. But Keats felt a conviction that
this heaven of immortal passion can be entered only through an
intensity of experience in this life, only by a mystic entrance into
the essence of that beauty which here fades; for we shall each be

[12] *Paradise Lost,* VIII. 452-89.

allotted an immortality of that degree of passion that our earthly
careers have attained. Therefore,

> O for a Life of Sensations rather than of Thoughts! It is
> "a Vision in the form of Youth" a Shadow of reality to
> come—and this consideration has further convinced me for
> it has come as auxiliary to another favorite Speculation of
> mine, that we shall enjoy ourselves here after by having what
> we called happiness on Earth repeated in a finer tone and so
> repeated. And yet such a fate can only befall those who
> delight in Sensation rather than hunger as you do after
> Truth. Adam's dream will do here and seems to be a convic-
> tion that Imagination and its empyreal reflection is the same
> as human Life and its Spiritual repetition.

Briefly, a life of sensations provides us with experiences of beauty
that we shall later enjoy under those immortal conditions that
Keats called "truth"; it foreshadows in the transitory the "reality" to come. Therefore, if we could, by a supernal power, rise
to perceive the empyreal reflection of what our merely human
imaginations create for us, we would be perceiving the spiritual
repetition of our human intensities, and hence our immortal
existence.

Such a supernal power is granted by the transcendent occasion
of St. Agnes' Eve, and thus Madeline's dream-vision, like Adam's,
has carried her beyond the "bar / That keeps us from our homes
ethereal." So far has she been transported by the empyreal reflection of her imagination, and therefore so deep is she in the spiritual
repetition of her earthly happiness, that her bond with the mortal
world is drawn thin and nearly severed: hers was

> *a midnight charm*
> *Impossible to melt as iced stream;*   (282-83)

and it seemed that Porphyro

> *never, never could redeem*
> *From such a stedfast spell his lady's eyes.*   (286-87)

When, therefore, Madeline is awakened from her divine vision, her capacity to perceive both human life and the spiritual repetition of it that her transcendent dream has divulged allows her to experience simultaneously both the mortal and the immortal. Ideally, this sensory-visionary state should correspond to the nature of heaven's bourne, where the human and the ethereal, beauty and truth, are one. The mortal Porphyro presented to her senses and the ideal Porphyro of her vision should fuse mystically into an immortality of passionate experience, as warmly human as the one and yet as immutable as the other. The consummation of Madeline's equivocal perceptions should be the experience of a love that is forever panting and forever young.

But the poem is tending for the moment to follow the downward course of the " Ode on a Grecian Urn " and " La Belle Dame Sans Merci ": in the mortal world beauty does not exist as truth, and although human life is like its spiritual repetition in kind, it is widely different in degree. Therefore the intrusion of mortality is threatening to dispel the ideal vision, exactly as the recollection of the ravages of human passions dispelled the beauty-truth of the urn's frieze, and exactly as the whisperings of death-bound mortality called the knight out of the elfin grot. The difference between the mortal Porphyro and the visionary Porphyro—human life and its spiritual repetition—is too great to allow the two to coalesce into a human-ethereal identity; and consequently the sight of mortality was to Madeline " a painful change, that nigh expell'd / The blisses of her dream so pure and deep " (300–301). In her vision of immortality Porphyro's eyes were " spiritual and clear," but now she finds them " sad," sadness being inextricable from human existence. " How chang'd thou art! how pallid, chill, and drear!" she adds (311), for Porphyro, like the knight-at-arms and his fellow mortals, is death-pale with the pallor, chill, and dreariness inherent in the nature of mortality. And this perishing that man calls " living " has become especially vivid to her because she has seen it in the light of the spiritual repetition of human happiness. Therefore Madeline pleads,

> *Give me that voice again, my Porphyro,*
> *Those looks immortal, those complainings dear!*
> *Oh leave me not in this eternal woe,*
> *For if thou diest, my Love, I know not where to go.*

The words " immortal " and " eternal " are diametrical opposites here and correspond to the difference we have encountered in the " Ode on a Grecian Urn " between the dimensionless essence of time and a plenitude of dimensional time. Immortality belongs to heaven's bourne and describes Porphyro's spiritual appearance; immortality has to do with a realm where existence is not merely endless, but where death and time are irrelevancies. Eternality, on the other hand, is an earthly measurement, and the two words underscore Madeline's precarious balance between these two conditions—the atemporality that belongs to her vision of Porphyro and the temporality in which the earthly Porphyro exists.

It is, however, entirely in the language of her ideal vision, not of her sensory perception, that she expresses a fear lest Porphyro die, for her extraordinary dream has revealed the immortal, or deathless Porphyro; although her awakened eyes are now looking at what man calls the " living " Porphyro, from the perspective of her dream-vision, which coexists with her sensory perception, he is taking on the pallid, chill, and drear form of mortality, i. e., deathliness. His dying, therefore, is a withdrawal from immortality, which is an everness of living, into a worldly existence, the active principle of which is to die. Madeline's fear is that hers will be the fate of the knight-at-arms: the elfin grot will turn out to be merely the cold hill side; mortality will summon her back from her insight into the beauty-truth to come and leave her only a world in which man forever repeats his one mortal drama, a progress from town to sacrificial altar.

Madeline's dream, then, is Adam's—but her awakening is, for the moment, far different. By spiritual grace she has experienced in a finer tone what she has called happiness on earth. And yet, she has not awakened from her dream to find it truth, for in the mutable world into which she is awakening, beauty is not truth, passions are not immortal, eyes are not spiritual and clear. Only in heaven's bourne do men of sensations awaken to find that their empyreal imaginings are true. Hence Madeline is being called back to an existence that is necessarily sorrowful and to a world where every knight-at-arms is " woe-begone." The impending dissolution of her vision through the summons to mutability and decay causes her to

> weep,
> *And moan forth witless words with many a sigh;*
> *While still her gaze on Porphyro would keep.*
> (302-304)

So, too, foreshadowing the imminent return of the knight to the mutable world because of the inability of mortals to remove the mutable from their visions, la belle dame " wept and sigh'd full sore " when she and the knight arrived at the elfin grot.

In one sense, then, Madeline's double vision is an analogue of a heaven's bourne that for the moment refuses to come about because her ideal dream and her sensory perception refuse to coalesce. But in another sense Madeline is herself the ideal and coldly chaste steadfastness of the bright star which, when animated with an exquisite intensity of warm human passion, becomes the oxymoronic nature of life's spiritual repetition.[18] For the magic of St. Agnes' Eve has transformed her into a Cynthia, the completed form of all completeness. In her chastity, her visionary power, and the

---

[18] " Bright star ! would I were steadfast as thou art."

spiritual purity that St. Agnes' Eve has bestowed upon her, she is the immutability of the life to come, but not its human intensity. She is " St. Agnes' charmed maid " (192), " a mission'd spirit " (193), " all akin / To spirits of the air " (201–202), " so pure a thing, so free from mortal taint " (225) ; she seems a saint, " a splendid angel, newly drest, / Save wings, for heaven " (222–24). Caught up in her dream-vision, she is sheltered alike from joy and pain (240), those complementary passions that attend upon all man's experiences while he is on earth. In withdrawing into her own self in sleep she becomes the perfection of form, " As though a rose should shut, and be a bud again " (243) ; she is not the full-blown rose giving up its fragrance, just as living is an expenditure of life, but a self-contained and unexpended power with need of nothing beyond itself, an emblem of Becoming eternally captured, and therefore perfect and immutable. Consequently, the merely human Porphyro worships her as his " heaven," while he sees himself as her " eremite " (277). She is, in short, the condition of immortality at heaven's bourne, its freedom from time, space, and selfhood.

But at heaven's bourne love is not simply forever *to be* enjoyed ; it is not immutable simply because it is never experienced. It is at the same time forever *being* enjoyed. And it is the human Porphyro, not graced by the supernal power of St. Agnes' Eve, who is the human passion that Madeline will raise to an immortality. He must so " delight in Sensation " that a " Spiritual repetition " of his earthly happiness will be available to him.

In the two poems we have already examined, Keats allowed the intrusion of the mutable world to dispel his vision of heaven. But in " The Eve of St. Agnes " he is concerned with pressing forward into the consequences of coalescing mortal experience and the condition of immortality, not with tracing the homeward journey of mortality to its habitual self, as he did in " La Belle Dame Sans Merci " and the " Ode on a Grecian Urn." Therefore the perception of the mortal Porphyro only " *nigh* expell'd / The blisses " of Madeline's dream. Having threatened to recall Madeline to mortality, Keats now reverses his strategy. Granted that in this world beauty is not truth, let us assume, he proposes, that mortality could rise to such heights that the difference between the two Porphyro's would be blotted out because the intensity of his mortal passions would then correspond to the intensity of his spiritual repetition. Madeline would no longer be torn between truth and beauty, for the two would coincide; and the ideal Madeline and the human Porphyro could unite to experience the conditions of heaven. Granted this ideal situation, for which Keats himself yearned; granted what is beyond mortal capacity—into what transcendent wisdom could man then penetrate?

In the poem, therefore, a miracle is to be performed; and instead of being thrust back into humanity after the " many hours of toil and quest " (338) which make up man's effort to become one with his ideal and to achieve an identity of truth and beauty, Porphyro will succeed in order that the mystery into which man would thereby penetrate may be revealed. For this purpose he is " A famish'd pilgrim,—saved by miracle " (339). Since only an intensity of passion can lead to a future repetition in a finer tone of what we call happiness on earth, and since such a repetition is permitted only to one who delights in sensations, Porphyro must first arise " Beyond a mortal man impassion'd far " (316). The ambiguous syntax (Keats first wrote, " Impassioned far beyond a mortal man ") implies that Porphyro's passion remains human in its nature and yet is raised to superhuman intensity. Only in this manner can the gap between mortal and immortal be bridged, for Porphyro thereby is raising human passion to the " finer tone " in which it will be experienced hereafter. In this act Porphyro has become " ethereal " (318). The word, we have seen, is a favorite with Keats and usually describes the transfiguration of real things into values by means of ardor. By the straining of his passion Porphyro has become an "ethereal thing," a value that is the ultimate significance of his mortal self and its experiences. Now, and only now, beauty may be united with truth, the mortal with the ethereal, to become the eternity of passion that exists only in heaven's bourne:

> *Ethereal, flush'd, and like a throbbing star*
> *Seen mid the sapphire heaven's deep repose*
> *Into her dream he melted, as the rose*
> *Blendeth its odour with the violet,—*
> *Solution sweet.* (318-22)

The steadfastness of the bright star and the soft fall and swell of "love's ripening breast" have coalesced; or rather, to use the images of the stanza, the throbbing of the star has been absorbed into the repose of the sky. The mortal Porphyro has risen to such a degree of passionate ardor that it may now blend with the chaste immutability that Madeline has become by virtue of the grace of St. Agnes' Eve. By the blending of their powers Madeline and Porphyro are now experiencing the spiritual repetition of human life and can therefore move into its mystery, which is the pith of human life and with which human life strives to nourish itself. For lack of this spiritual nourishment the mortal Porphyro had been a "famish'd pilgrim" (339), just as for the same reason the death-pale mortals of "La Belle Dame Sans Merci" have starved lips. Madeline's dream has turned out to be Adam's after all; by a miracle she has awakened to find it truth.

While this immortality of passion is dramatically evolving in the foreground through the overt actions which melt the human ardor of Porphyro into the ideal constancy, the "deep repose," of Madeline's vision, a parallel development is also taking place in the background which not only infuses into the central drama a powerful tonal quality but also re-enacts symbolically the union of Porphyro and Madeline so as to expand the otherwise personal action to cosmic size and significance. Waiting to be led to Madeline, Porphyro remains in " a little moonlight room, / Pale, lattic'd, chill, and silent as a tomb " (112–13). There Angela tells him of Madeline's intention to observe the rites of St. Agnes' Eve, and as a result

> *Sudden a thought came like a full-blown rose,*
> *Flushing his brow, and in his pained heart*
> *Made purple riot.* (136-38)

These two symbols—cold and silvery pale moonlight, and the warmly sensuous ruddiness of purple and rose—correspond to the two conditions that are one in heaven's bourne. In the first room Porphyro is in the presence of the moonlight, but it is only lifeless and chill unless it is animated by the color of passion, the roseate sensuousness that at length is born in Porphyro. Silver and moonlight therefore hover about Madeline, the Cynthia of the poem, the eternal form with which human passion must blend. She carries " a silver taper " (194) which dies in the " pallid moonshine " of her own chamber (200) ; she wears a silver cross (221) ; and before Keats finally described her as a " splendid angel " (223) he tried " immortal angel " and " silvery angel." She is Porphyro's " silver shrine " (337), he her beauty's shield, " heart-shap'd and vermeil dyed " (336).

The silveriness and moonlight belong to the realm of pure being, the rich blushes of color to the realm of passionate becoming. Consequently, when Madeline enters her chamber the two colors begin to run together, interpenetrating to prefigure the act which will coalesce human and spiritual into a love that is " still to be enjoy'd." The chaste moonlight shines through the stained-glass windows, whose gorgeous colors are " Innumerable of stains and splendid dyes, / As are the tiger-moth's deep-damask'd wings "

(212–13) so that the two colors partake of each other as though cosmic forces had shaped at an all-pervasive level the heaven's bourne that Madeline and Porphyro are to find at the human level. In this silver-red, or chaste-sensuous atmospheric fusion, the subsequent action of the spirit-sense union is bathed. The cold, virginal light of the " wintry moon " throws a warm roseate stain on Madeline's white breast; it makes rose-bloom fall on her hands, which are clasped in holy prayer; it covers the silvery spirituality of her cross with the luxurious purple of amethyst (217–21).

The fusion continues to permeate the setting as Porphyro prepares for the union. In the " dim, silver twilight " he places a cloth of " woven crimson, gold, and jet " (253–56); he fills with fruit golden dishes and baskets of " wreathed silver " (271–73); and lustrous salvers gleaming in the moonlight and golden-fringed carpets appear as adjacent images (284–85). As the bloody dyes have become the sensuous vitality of the virginal moonlight, Porphyro now rises to ethereal passions to melt into Madeline's spiritual vision. The scents of the rose and the chaste violet dissolve into each other (320–22). The union having been consummated and the conditions of heaven's bourne having been attained, the supernatural grace is no longer needed or pertinent. Porphyro and Madeline have fashioned their own heaven: " St. Agnes' moon hath set " (324).

iii

As the poem was passing through its various manuscript forms, Keats added and later deleted a stanza between what are now stanzas six and seven. Stanza six describes some of the ceremonies required of virgins on St. Agnes' Eve if they are to have their visions of delight, and the deleted stanza then added:

> 'Twas said her future lord would there appear
> Offering as sacrifice—all in the dream—
> Delicious food even to her lips brought near:

Viands and wine and fruit and sugar'd cream,
To touch her palate with the fine extreme
Of relish: then soft music heard; and then
More pleasures followed in a dizzy stream
Palpable almost: then to wake again
Warm in the virgin morn, no weeping Magdalen.

Had the stanza been retained, the reader would be better prepared for Porphyro's otherwise unmotivated actions in Madeline's chamber and for some of Angela's bustlings. But even so, the critic would have been required to face the problems the stanza introduces. Almost uniformly the commentators have agreed with William Michael Rossetti on the irrelevance of the feast later in the poem: " One of the few subsidiary incidents introduced into ' The Eve of St. Agnes ' is that the lover Porphyro, on emerging from his hiding-place while his lady is asleep, produces from a cupboard and marshals to sight a large assortment of appetizing eatables. Why he did this no critic and no admirer has yet been able to divine." [14] Most significant, the omitted stanza outlines the only important action Porphyro engages in prior to his union with Madeline, except for his passage from one chamber to another. Even if these otherwise irrelevant actions concerning food and music were requirements of the legend, as Keats pretends, why does he give them such significance in a narrative remarkable for its unilinear direction? Why, when the other rituals are only lightly touched upon, does Keats have Angela speak particularly of the food and the lute? and why does he then dwell upon these two rituals when Porphyro is in Madeline's chamber?

But, in fact, the details outlined in the omitted stanza have not been found to be part of the legend. The folk tradition does require that the virgin lie supine, look not behind her, speak not a word, retire fasting, and look to heaven for aid; however, there is no

[14] *Life of John Keats* (London, 1887), 183.

evidence that it requires a feast and music. We must search, instead, for some compelling reason why Keats introduced more than the narrative itself calls for. Once again, it is clear, he has reshaped a legend in order to weave through it the series of increasing intensities of the pleasure thermometer that he understood to be the necessary means of spiritual elevation before one may enter the dynamically static heaven Madeline and Porphyro are about to create for themselves. The rich foods correspond to the level of sensuous essence, and Keats is careful to underscore the sensory vigor he means to convey: " To touch her palate with the fine extreme / Of relish." Then music; and at last, since the subject has now stepped into " a sort of oneness," the great range of " happinesses " made up of love and friendship. These essences are to be so strenuously envisioned that they are " Palpable almost "— sensuous and yet spiritual, real and yet visionary, beautiful and yet true.

We can now understand why, after Porphyro has told Angela his plan to enact physically the visions of Madeline's dreams—that is, to perform in human reality what Madeline is experiencing at a transcendent level—Angela is quick to reply:

> ' It shall be as thou wishest . . .
> ' All cates and dainties shall be stored there
> ' Quickly on this feast-night: by the tambour frame
> ' Her own lute thou wilt see. . . .' (172-75)

Porphyro has recognized that the dream-vision for which Madeline is preparing is an ascent to the " chief intensity," to the spiritual repetition of what we call happiness on earth; and therefore the feast and the music represent the sensuous and imaginative entrances into essence before the spiritual entrance through love. Consequently, when Porphyro passes into Madeline's chamber he first prepares the remarkably rich foods, which are heaped upon one another in such profusion as to leave the reader glutted with the luxury:

> *a heap*
> *Of candied apple, quince, and plum, and gourd*
> *With jellies soother than the creamy curd,*
> *And lucent syrops, tinct with cinnamon;*
> *Manna and dates, in argosy transferr'd*
> *From Fez; and spiced dainties, every one,*
> *From silken Samarcand to cedar'd Lebanon.* (264-70)

The manuscript shows that the stanza gave the poet a great deal of trouble, for his purpose is not to fashion a menu or wallow in a luxury of feelings, but to engage the whole range of the senses in their extremes. An exquisite sense of taste, touch, sight, and smell is excited to produce a kind of synaesthetic response; it is the essence of the sensuous faculty itself that Keats means to call upon, and nothing less than " the fine extreme of relish " will do to lead one to the final intensity of heaven's bourne.

Porphyro now advances to the next stage, the essence to which the imagination finds its way, by taking Madeline's lute and playing to her the ancient ditty " La Belle Dame Sans Merci." The ballad is especially appropriate since it tells of the failure of human powers to remain in the elfin grot and of the necessary return to death-pale and woe-begone mortality; and thus the warning it holds out disturbs Madeline's vision. She utters " a soft moan " and her eyes are " affrayed." But at the same time the disturbance also causes Madeline, although retaining her vision, to awaken to physical reality so that she is no longer self-contained, locked in the self-sufficiency of her vision; and she is thus no longer the unknown, but, as Endymion called Cynthia, a " known Unknown," [15] " an unknown—but no more," an ideal now accessible to Porphyro so that he may melt into her vision. While she remained in her visionary self-sufficiency she was both unknown and unknowable to

[15] *Endymion*, II. 739.

Porphyro, and the intensity of his human passions could only torment as he yearned for the spiritual immutability that would fix
them forever:

> *Open thine eyes, for meek St. Agnes' sake,*
> *Or I shall drowse beside thee, so my soul doth ache.*

(278-79)

His passionate experience is destroying his selfhood, but no essence
is available into which his self may pass; and hence he can feel
only a swooning of his senses.

iv

Until now we have been examining mainly the actions of
Porphyro and Madeline that take place in Madeline's chamber, and
they constitute an ascent of the ladder of intensities and a formation
of the mystic oxymoron which is the spiritual repetition of the
" happiness " of human life. Let us consider now Porphyro's other
actions. Before he enters the chamber he has ridden across the
moor to the castle; has stood outside the castle, where he was
hidden by the buttress; has entered the castle and been led by
Angela to a little room " silent as a tomb," where he has learned of
Madeline's plan and fashioned his own; and finally has been led to
a closet of Madeline's chamber. This pattern of events, abstracted
from the poem, appears to form some sort of progression as Porphyro moves from the outer darkness and cold to the warmth of the
castle and then ascends in stages from the " level chambers " (32)
to the " paradise " (244) of Madeline's room.

Doors, chambers, and mansions seem to have possessed especially important symbolic values in Keats' mind. The mind has
a " cage-door " [16] or a casement " To let the warm Love in "; [17] it

---

[16] " Fancy," 7.   [17] " Ode to Psyche," 66-67.

is made up of " cerebral apartments " or is an " enchanted palace." [18] The imagination is a monastery, the poet its monk.[19] Pan
is the " Dread opener of the mysterious doors / Leading to universal knowledge." [20] The doors of heaven " appear'd to open " for
Endymion's visionary flight to Cynthia; [21] and Apollo's chariot
waits " at the doors of heaven." [22] The " enchanted Portals " of
heaven open wide for the poet.[23] The nightingale makes casements
magic, and in the " Enchanted Castle " the doors " all look as if
they oped themselves." [24] These and other passages are suggestive
enough to prompt the question of whether the apartments, doors,
and portals of " The Eve of St. Agnes " embody a value beyond
their narrative function.

Less than a year before he wrote his romance, Keats had been
speculating on the significance of Wordsworth's poetry and attempting to determine the height that Wordsworth had attained in
the range of values. By using as his scale the pattern of life that
Wordsworth had outlined in " Tintern Abbey," Keats was also
hoping to see more vividly the stage of human values that he himself had grown to make central in his art. In May, 1818, approximately eight months before he began to compose " The Eve of St.
Agnes," he wrote to John Hamilton Reynolds that he had been
turning over in his mind whether Wordsworth " has an extended
vision or a circumscribed grandeur."

And to be more explicit and to show you how tall I stand
by the giant, I will put down a simile of human life as far as
I now perceive it; that is, to the point to which I say we both

---

[18] Letter to George and Georgiana Keats, February 14-May 3, 1819.
[19] Letter to Shelley, August 16, 1820.
[20] *Endymion*, I. 288-89.
[21] *Ibid.*, 581-82.
[22] *Ibid.*, III. 959.
[23] " To my Brother George," 30.
[24] " To J. H. Reynolds, Esq.," 49.

have arrived at—Well—I compare human life to a large
Mansion of Many Apartments, two of which I can only
describe, the doors of the rest being as yet shut upon me.
The first we step into we call the infant or thoughtless
Chamber, in which we remain as long as we do not think—
We remain there a long while, and notwithstanding the doors
of the second Chamber remain wide open, showing a bright
appearance, we care not to hasten to it; but are at length
imperceptibly impelled by the awakening of this thinking
principle within us—we no sooner get into the second Chamber, which I shall call the Chamber of Maiden-Thought, than
we become intoxicated with the light and the atmosphere,
we see nothing but pleasant wonders, and think of delaying
there for ever in delight: However among the effects this
breathing is father of is that tremendous one of sharpening
one's vision into the heart and nature of Man—of convincing
one's nerves that the world is full of Misery and Heartbreak,
Pain, Sickness and oppression—whereby this Chamber of
Maiden Thought becomes gradually darken'd and at the same
time on all sides of it many doors are set open—but all dark—
all leading to dark passages—We see not the ballance of good
and evil. We are in a Mist. *We* are now in that state—We
feel the " burden of the Mystery," To this Point was Wordsworth come, as far as I can conceive when he wrote " Tintern
Abbey " and it seems to me that his Genius is explorative of
those dark Passages. Now if we live, and go on thinking,
we too shall explore them.[25]

The stages outlined here correspond roughly to the three implicit
in " Tintern Abbey ": a period of thoughtless animal pleasure
without even awareness of the pleasure, one of consciousness of
emotional power, and at last a perception of the " still, sad music
of humanity " which brings a sense of " something far more deeply
interfused " and consequently lightens " the burden of the mystery."
The relation Keats' letter has to Wordsworth's pattern of life and
of the growth of the poetic mind reveals how deeply indebted

[25] Letter to Reynolds, May 3, 1818.

Keats was to the older poet for his own most profound inquiry into the meaning of human existence.

In the career of Porphyro, then, Keats has incorporated his semi-Wordsworthian vision of life as a progress from mere animal existence to an understanding of the mystery that permeates life; and the castle is that Mansion of Many Apartments in which human existence plays out its part. When Porphyro arrives at the castle he stands beside the portal doors, " Buttress'd from moonlight " (77), merely hoping that he may gaze on Madeline, the beauty for which he longs. In this infant existence of his spirit, he is shut off from the light of the ideal moon which shines on mortal things to reveal them in their immortal aspects; and consequently in the " tedious hours " (79) which make up life he can do no more than yearn for an entrance into existence so as to experience its riches: " Perchance speak, kneel, touch, kiss " (80–81). Shaded from the visionary splendor by the buttress of human life, he can have only a sensory impulse towards the perfect mortal beauty and can expect little more than that he might gaze upon it and worship it " But for one moment in the tedious hours " of his mortal days.

But this worldly beauty towards which he is impelled before he enters the castle is not transfigured by the spiritual light of the moon-goddess, and hence he has no understanding of the meaning of his impulse. However, having entered the castle of human life, he quickly circumvents the level chambers of the " mansion foul " (89) in which life is a distracting game played for its own sake and where the " barbarian hordes " resent all that he represents. Led by Angela to the first chamber, he is there bathed in the light of ideality, but, since the intensity of human passion is lacking, the room is only " Pale, lattic'd, chill, and silent as a tomb " (113). In this " thoughtless Chamber, in which we remain as long as we do not think," Porphyro merely exists, resting in childlike innocence and awe, " Like puzzled urchin," while Angela tells of Madeline's plan. In this spiritual adolescence he is driven by an impulse of his senses, but not by a consciousness of his sensuous desires. Angela's revelation, however, arouses him from the thoughtlessness which allows him to remain in the first chamber, and knowledge of Madeline's intention to experience the spiritual repetition of earthly happiness awakens the thinking principle within him and impels him to seek out Madeline's chamber: " Sudden a thought came like a full-blown rose, . . . then doth he propose / A stratagem " (136–39). The consciousness of his sensuous powers drives him then to Madeline's chamber—the " Chamber of Maiden-Thought."

The spiritual ascent that is implicit in Porphyro's progress from chamber to chamber becomes clear by the fact that he remains in a closet adjacent to Madeline's chamber, for Keats originally called this closet a " Purgatory sweet " and retained his description of the chamber itself as a " paradise." In other words, Porphyro has transcended the merely human life of the " level chambers " and is now in the purgatory to which he must move before he can attain the heavenly repetition of earthly happiness. From this purgatory he can look upon " all that he may attain," " love's own domain." [26] In the Chamber of Maiden-Thought we are intoxicated with the light and atmosphere and see nothing but pleasant wonders; and thus Porphyro looks upon the disrobing Madeline, the ideal revealing its naked perfection. Entranced, breathless, he is wholly engaged in the splendor of the revelation, just as the knight-at-arms sees nothing but the fairy's child because his self is being absorbed; and because each man reaches this stage only within himself as an inward experience of his total self, Porphyro is seeing the " beauty unespied," " in close secrecy " (163, 166). Here in the Chamber of Maiden-Thought the ascent of the scale of intensities is acted out, and Porphyro and Madeline unite in a mystic blending of

[26] Stanza 21, variant.

mortality and immortality, chastity and passion, the moonlight of perfect form and the ruddiness of intense experience. They have attained the stage where life's self is nourished by its own pith, and they can now progress into the mystery that is the core of life.

In the " Ode on a Grecian Urn " and in " La Belle Dame Sans Merci," Keats had found that merely human life cannot continue to experience the life that our imaginations tell us is to come. However, the points on which he tipped the web of " The Eve of St. Agnes " are an hypothesis. Suppose we could penetrate into heaven's bourne by elevating our human passions to an intensity that would allow them to blend with a changeless immortality and thus be spiritually transfigured—suppose we could experience our heaven on earth—to what sphery sessions would we be admitted? One of the effects of the splendid vision we perceive in the Chamber of Maiden-Thought is " that tremendous one of sharpening one's vision into the heart and nature of Man—of convincing one's nerves that the world is full of Misery and Heartbreak, Pain, Sickness and oppression." Hence, when the union has been consummated and the lovers are experiencing the spiritual repetition of life, the supernal power that has granted them the vision is now no longer relevant. The moon has set and the chamber has grown dark because the mystery to which they are now admitted can be known to man only as a darkness. This is not the darkness of ignorance that surrounded Porphyro before his entrance into the castle, but the darkness that Keats invoked in his sonnet " Why did I laugh to-night? " It is the mist in which man's knowledge of heaven, hell, and his own self are wrapped.[27] It is the darkness which God made " his secret place " so that " his pavilion round about him were dark waters and thick clouds of the skies." [28] The moon has made possible a transcendence of human life in order that the

[27] " Written upon the Top of Ben Nevis."
[28] Psalms xviii. 11.

lovers may progress, not to light, but to the dark secret beyond the castle which confines them to the activities of mortal life. Hence they find " a darkling way " (355), the " dark passages " to which the Chamber of Maiden-Thought leads. Hearing no human sound, they escape into the mysterious elfin storm which is " Of haggard seeming, but a boon indeed " (343-44), the dark secret of life, the " vision into the heart and nature of Man," which terrifies sublunary mortals, but which guards one from the savagery of the world and allows him to " see into the life of things." Only to this point is Keats willing to go; he feels the burden of the mystery, but he is not yet ready to explore the dark passages through which Porphyro and Madeline are now travelling.

Having experienced the spiritual repetition of human happiness, Porphyro and Madeline are no longer active powers. Of his friend Dilke, Keats wrote that he will never arrive at a truth because he is always striving after it; [29] and Coleridge, he complained, will " let go by a fine isolated verisimilitude caught from the Penetralium of mystery, from being incapable of remaining Content with half knowledge." [30] One enters the mystery, not by wilfull probing, but by allowing himself to be absorbed into it. Once man has experienced the wonders of the Chamber of Maiden-Thought and gained insight into the agony of human life, the mystery unfolds itself; and an effort to pry open its doors would only shut them more tightly. Therefore, in the poem the light grows dark, and the mystery opens its own doors upon itself: " on all sides of it," as the letter to Reynolds says, " many doors are set open." So, too, Pan, being a knowable " unknown," the link between heaven and earth, the spirit that makes earth ethereal, is himself the " Dread opener of the mysterious doors / Leading to universal knowledge ";

[29] Letter to George and Georgiana Keats, September 17-27, 1819.
[30] Letter to George and Thomas Keats, December 21, 1817.

for he is a symbol of the mystic sense-spirit union the lovers have fashioned.

With the enactment of this theme of passive absorption Keats now rounds out the conclusion of his romance. In one of the most dramatically controlled passages in English poetry he melts the lovers into a spaceless, timeless, selfless realm of mystery, exactly as the poet of the " Ode on a Grecian Urn " and the knight-at-arms were selflessly assimilated into a visionary heaven. At first we perceive the lovers preparing to escape into the storm that lies beyond human existence; they themselves are the object of our attention as we see them moving down the wide stairs. They act directly before us in the historical past. Then, almost imperceptibly they are gradually released from dimensions. First they tend to fade as active powers. After having been vividly active before us and the center of our attention, they govern little directly in the last three stanzas; in the main the action passes from them into the control of the things that surround them—the lamp, arras, carpets, bloodhound, chains, key, and door; and the sense of their active presence is further dimmed by the introduction of the passive verb: " In all the house was heard no human sound " (356).

They further lose selfhood and palpable existence as the reader becomes identified with them, moving in them through the passageways and seeing, no longer the lovers, but what could be seen by them in their progress—the flickering of the lamp, the fluttering of the arras, the rising of the carpets with the wind. The camera is no longer focused on the lovers, but has become their eyes so that as we watch what the lovers see, they themselves may steal away from our mode of existence. When next we glance at them they have become indistinct and have blurred into insubstantial things; their movement is the insubstantial essence of movement, not a human act, and they themselves have become visionary:

They glide, like phantoms, into the wide hall;
Like phantoms, to the iron porch, they glide. (361-62)

Meanwhile, the narrative becomes not merely one of the histori-cal past, an action completed at some specific date in the past, but also one that is both immediate and universal; and this effect is controlled by the subtle manipulation of the past tense and the his-torical present. At first all the action is expressed by the past tense: the lovers " found " their way, the lamp " was flickering," the arras " flutter'd." At this point Keats mingles past and present: the lovers " glide," the porter " lay," the bloodhound " rose " and " shook " his hide, and his eye " owns " an inmate. The inter-mingling of tenses is not careless, but nicely shapes a confusion of the sense of time by making the reader teeter between past and present. Both tenses are appropriate to a description of past events, for the historical present (" glide " and " owns ") gives a sense of presentness to past events; but the effect of the intermingling of the tenses is to bring the action out of a fixed position in time and dim all impression of temporality: the lovers seem to glide this very moment before us, and yet they have left the castle in the remote past. However, the introduction of the present tense blurs the sense of time through even greater ambiguity, for it may be the historical present, the immediate present, or the universal present; and indeed in the poem it is all these, and all at the same time. Hence it is this multivalent present tense that emerges from the intermingling of the past and present, and governs the account of all the final action: the bolts " slide," the chains " lie " silent, the key " turns," and the door " groans "; and the previous confusion of the temporal refer-ence now causes these present tenses to place the actions outside the context of time: the chains lay silent in the past, lie silent now, and indeed always lie silent.

With this evaporation of time, all human agency also vanishes as the lovers fade entirely from the scene. We do not see them as they make the bolts of the castle door slide open, nor are we the lovers seeing their own action of moving the bolts; for the effect of one's arrival at the border of the mystery is that "many doors *are set* open." No agency at all slides the bolts and chains, and yet the bolts and chains slide, and the door groans on its hinges—and Porphyro and Madeline are outside the human order, beyond the "mysterious doors" that lead to "universal knowledge." The lovers are wholly caught up in timelessness and no longer exist as human actors. "And they are gone": the action of the participle ("gone") belongs to the past, but the adjectival use of the participle here divests it of its verbal quality; it is a description, a quality of being, not an act, and therefore it implies no agency. The lovers' being gone is outside time and activity. The poet now catches up this sense of timelessness and swells it by having endless ages spin away before our time-bound minds:

> And they are gone: ay, ages long ago
> These lovers fled away into the storm.   (370-71)

No longer are Porphyro and Madeline human actors, or even phantoms, but the selfless spirit of man forever captured in the dimensionless mystery beyond our mortal vision.

The symbolizing act that takes place in the first three stanzas of "La Belle Dame Sans Merci" is performed at the conclusion of the romance. In the ballad Keats began by shaping image and value until he had dramatized the fact that the poem is symbolic. Here, at the conclusion of the romance, the vital current of the actors flows beyond them while they are being refined out of existence. The vitality has impersonalized itself to become vital values beyond and independent of the actors who gave them their impetus.

V

In the background of the narrative we have been tracing there are three other sets of characters who, by their contrast with the warmth, passion, and ardor of the youthful lovers, not only give the central narrative an artistic depth, but also act out their various roles in the Mansion of Many Apartments to reveal other ways in which life may be lived. The beadsman, who surrounds the entire poem with a framework of chill, plays his part in the outer passages of the castle. His movement takes him along the chapel aisles and to his place of penance; he only skirts the chambers in which the revelry takes place. Hearing the music of the gay dance, he is tempted to move towards the joys of life; but " already had his deathbell rung " (22), and he continues his way outside the central chambers, avoiding the sensuous intensities of life, despite the temptation. The beadsman, then, is eschewing the vigors of human experience and has dedicated himself to heaven alone. He is the chill of that life which avoids sensuous warmth: his breath is " frosted " (6), and he tells his rosary with numb fingers (5). He leads his mortal life only that he may put it aside; by praying for his soul's reprieve and grieving for sinners' sake he hopes to stifle his physical existence and thereby exalt and assure his spiritual salvation.

But the enjoyment in a finer tone hereafter of what we have called happiness on earth is a fate that " can only befall those who delight in Sensation rather than hunger as you do after Truth," Keats wrote to his clerical friend Benjamin Bailey.[31] Adam's dream does not apply to those who, like the beadsman, hunger after " truth." Even the beadsman's breath symbolizes the misdirection of his life: his breath (spirit) " Seem'd taking flight for heaven, without a death " (8). But death, Keats tells us elsewhere, is " Life's high meed " [32]—the final intensity that climaxes the intensities of human existence and unites life with its proper pith. For the man of sensations, human experiences are a progress to

[31] Letter to Bailey, November 22, 1817.
[32] " Why did I laugh to-night? "

heaven's bourne, and death is the last and most vigorous of these experiences.

The beadsman's, however, is " Another way " (25) ; he hopes, not to make sensuous earthly existence an ascent to a spiritual repetition, but to dodge life and its high meed, death, and to be as oblivious to the senses as his fingers are numb with the cold. He would grasp " truth " alone, without beauty, in one leap. For such a life which avoids sensations there is no spiritual repetition in a finer tone; and the beadsman, after thousand futile aves, becomes only the mutable physical substance that belongs to this world: " For aye unsought for slept among his ashes cold " (378). The irony is that on the very night that the lovers are caught up in the mystery through the fixing of exquisite passion in an immortality, the beadsman, seeking to subdue the flesh to the spirit, becomes only meaningless, lifeless matter among the very ashes that sym- bolize the meaninglessness of the mortal body. In this light we can understand somewhat better why Keats felt an impulse—not dictated by a sense of poetic effect—to make even more grotesque and gruesome the beadsman's fate, and at one point in the composi- tion of the poem made the last few lines read:

> *and with face deform*
> *The beadsman stiffen'd, 'twixt a sigh and laugh*
> *Ta'en sudden from his beads by one weak little cough.*

Originally Keats included between stanzas three and four another stanza that reveals the progression he intended in passing from the beadsman to the revelers and then to the lovers. After describing the beadsman's avoidance of the life of sensations he added:

> *But there are ears may hear sweet melodies,*
> *And there are eyes to brighten festivals,*
> *And there are feet for nimble minstrelsies,*
> *And many a lip that for the red wine calls.—*
> *Follow, then follow to the illumined halls,*

Follow me youth—and leave the eremite—
Give him a tear—then trophied banneral
And many a brilliant tasseling of light
Shall droop from arched ways this high baronial night.

Clearly the meagre and wan beadsman is to be thrust aside as one who considers the world " ' a vale of tears ' from which we are to be redeemed by a certain arbitrary interposition of God and taken to Heaven—What a little circumscribed straightened notion ! " [33] For such a misguided view we may feel a touch of sadness—" Give him a tear "—but we are to move instead to a somewhat higher view of life by an entrance into its strenuosity and riches.

And yet, the revelers in the hall, the converse of the beadsman, cannot perceive beyond the limits of their momentary excitement. In the " level chambers " they seek pleasure and agitation merely as an end in itself and hope to find happiness on earth so that " the whole troubles of life which are now frittered away in a series of years, would then be accumulated for the last days of a being who instead of hailing [Death's] approach, would leave this world as Eve left Paradise." [34] Therefore these, too,

let us wish away,
And turn, sole-thoughted, to one Lady there.   (41–42)

Originally, Keats made even more vivid his rejection of the revelers as he leads the reader through the increasing stages from beadsman, to revelers, to the lovers. Of the revelers he wrote:

Ah what are they? the idle pulse scarce stirs[.]
The Muse should never make the spirit gay;
Away, bright dulness, laughing fools away,—
And let me tell of one sweet lady there.

Thus the beadsman and the baron's guests are antitheses: the first

[33] Letter to George and Georgiana Keats, February 14–May 3, 1819.
[34] *Ibid.*

avoids life for soul; the latter neglect soul for life alone. For this
very reason the beadsman is irrelevant to the lovers and moves
about the periphery of the castle; but the baron and his guests are
hostile to them. By being unable to rise above the confines of
mortality and by remaining in the glowing " level " chambers sheltered from the gleam of the ideal moon, they are the death-pale
kings and princes who warn that " La Belle Dame sans Merci
/ Hath thee in thrall! "; and thus they conduct a feud against all
that Porphyro represents:

> *For him, those chambers held barbarian hordes,*
> *Hyena foemen, and hot-blooded lords,*
> *Whose very dogs would execrations howl*
> *Against his lineage.* (85–88)

The revelers engage in only the petty passions of the world:
" whisperers in anger, or in sport; / 'Mid looks of love, defiance,
hate, and scorn " (68-69) ; and only because " her heart was otherwhere " (62) could Madeline fulfill the rites of St. Agnes' Eve
and experience the spiritual repetition of life. It is this world of
the revelers that is always threatening to obtrude itself upon visions
of a love that is still to be enjoyed, and thereby to withdraw man
to the cold hill side. Even in the midst of Madeline's dream-vision
in the paradise of her chamber and in the midst of Porphyro's
preparations for the union, the noisiness of the mortal world
promises to reduce all to mere flesh-and-blood mutability:

> *O for some drowsy Morphean amulet!*
> *The boisterous, midnight, festive clarion,*
> *The kettle-drum, and far-heard clarionet,*
> *Affray his [Porphyro's] ears, though but in dying tone:—*
> *The hall door shuts again, and all the noise is gone.*
>
> (257–61)

For this life of the senses alone, Keats cannot restrain his
contempt. The " barbarian hordes " are " bloated wassaillers "

(346) who, being " Drown'd all in Rhenish and the sleepy mead,"
do not have " ears to hear, or eyes to see " the passage of the lovers
from the castle of mortality into the mystery of the elfin storm
(348-49). Consequently, the dreams of the baron and his guests—
" the whole blood-thirsty race " (99)—unlike Madeline's dream,
are only of the world in which all things decay. Instead of rising
by dream-vision to the spiritual repetition of human life, they can
dream only of human life, whose central principle is its deathliness:

> That night the Baron dreamt of many a woe,
> And all his warrior-guests, with shade and form
> Of witch, and demon, and large coffin-worm,
> Were long be-nightmar'd. (372–75)

Similarly, the inability of the knight-at-arms to remain at the
spiritual level of the elfin grot caused him to dream of " pale kings
and princes too, / Pale warriors, death-pale were they all."

Finally, both the drama and the theme of the poem are completed by Angela, who is a kind of norm of humanity. Like the
beadsman, she is careful of her soul; and yet she belongs to the
halls of revelry rather than the higher chambers, although she alone
is able to wander at will in both, unaffected by either. She will
never experience a love that is forever warm and still to be enjoyed
because she is devoid of both sensuous and spiritual intensity: she
is an " old beldame, weak in body and in soul " (90), a " poor,
weak, palsy-stricken, churchyard thing " (155). Madeline's desire
for a vision of her love is to Angela only a child's wish for an
unreal, deceptive dream-world; and consequently, failing to recognize it as an ascent to the sensuous-spiritual life of heaven, she
laughs " in the languid moon " (127), the light of the ideal, while
she tells Porphyro of the plan. Despite her interest in her own soul,
she can think of love only as the " mere commingling of passionate
breath," not knowing that it can produce " more than our search-

ing witnesseth "; [35] and thus she understands Porphyro's plan to result only from an evil sensual desire which must be purified by marriage.

Although she aids in Porphyro's enactment of the vision, the part she plays is almost too exacting for her feeble spirit and senses. She rises to a height beyond her strength, and so Madeline must lead her from the upper chambers down " To a safe level matting " (196), the level at which merely human existence is carried on and at which the baron and his guests seek worldly happiness. Since such weakness can never penetrate into the mystery, Angela, whose " passing-bell may ere the midnight toll " (156), on the very same night (we are left to assume) died " palsy-twitch'd, with meagre face deform " (375-76). Certainly a set of values that embrace more than esthetics drove Keats, as Richard Woodhouse reports, to alter " the last 3 lines to leave on the reader a sense of pettish disgust, by bringing Old Angela in (only) dead stiff & ugly.—He says he likes that the poem should leave off with this Change of Sentiment—it was what he aimed at, & was glad to find from my objections to it that he had succeeded." [36]

vi

It is, of course, a great convenience that we have Keats' letter on the Mansion of Many Apartments, for it is an elucidation of Porphyro's progress almost detail by detail. And yet, having made use of it, I should like to remove it from all considerations of the poem as poem.

Like a map, it has pointed out the journey we are to make, and should now be forgotten so that we may experience the countryside through which our journey takes us. At most, like Spenser's letter

[35] *Endymion*, I. 833-44.

[36] Richard Woodhouse's letter to Taylor, September 19-20, 1819; in *The Keats Circle*, ed. Hyder E. Rollins (Cambridge, Mass., 1948), I. 91.

to Raleigh, it stands outside the framework of the poem and explains to the conceptual mind the ideational equivalents of elements that, in the poem, perform artistic acts. To read the poem by continued reference to it is to imply that these artistic acts are consonant with, but not organically related to, their "meanings." Briefly, the letter is, at best, an extraction from the poem of its prose, or declarative, content. Yet even this is to grant too much to an historical accident, for only chance has made the letter available to us, and Keats wrote a self-contained poem, certainly never intending that his personal letter be superimposed on it. Poems, he said, should explain themselves "without any comment." [37] The danger is that the use of the letter distracts from the poem, for it suggests that the poem is to be read on two different levels: the literal level of the romantic narrative, and the ideational level of the letter, the two levels being related by point-to-point equivalences. In other words, the reading of the romance in the light of the prose statement suggests an allegorical interpretation.

In fact the letter is not at all indispensable. Let us consider for the moment a theme in "Sleep and Poetry." There Keats wrote that "life is but a day," "the rose's hope while yet unblown" (85, 90). It is but a moment in an unfolding into something greater; but the bud and the full-blown rose are not separable, for life here and life hereafter are not different in kind. To the man of sensations the postmortal life is a repetition of earthly "happiness" in a finer tone. The intensity of earthly experience must, then, be the means of progress into the mystery of our immortal experiences. Consequently, Keats planned first to

> *Write on my tablets all that was permitted,*
> *All that was for our human senses fitted.*
> *Then the events of this wide world I'd seize*

[37] Letter to George and Georgiana Keats, December 16, 1818-January 4, 1819.

Like a strong giant, and my spirit teaze
Till at its shoulders it should proudly see
Wings to find out an immortality. (79–84)

He would raise human experience to such intensity that it would
become the spiritual repetition of human life, exactly as Porphyro,
by rising "Beyond a mortal man impassion'd far," could then melt
into the immortality of Madeline and thus move into the mysterious
essence and origin of life. In the same early poem Keats then
restated more fully this pattern of a spiritual growth through
sensory experiences in the worldly Vale of Soul-Making. First he
would glut himself with the luxuries of beauty:

First the realm I'll pass
Of Flora, and old Pan: sleep in the grass,
Feed upon apples red, and strawberries,
And choose each pleasure that my fancy sees;
Catch the white-handed nymphs in shady places,
To woo sweet kisses from averted faces. (101–106)

Thereafter he would bid these joys farewell for a nobler life,
"Where I may find the agonies, the strife / Of human hearts"
(122-25). Imagination in the form of a charioteer now comes from
heaven to talk to the trees and mountains, the outward things of
nature, and to him "there soon appear / Shapes of delight, of
mystery, and fear" who "murmur, laugh, and smile, and weep"
(137-38, 142). These are the mysteries that reside in "the strife /
Of human hearts," and to these the charioteer, "Most awfully
intent," seems to listen (151-53). The charioteer, like the poet,
has progressed from things of the senses to the secret of the human
heart that experiences these sensations; and the poet wishes, "O
that I might know / All that he writes with such a hurrying glow"
(154-55).

The letter on the Mansion of Many Apartments is more explicit
and detailed, but the pattern is the same: a progress through sensation to the wonder of life, for since the life to come is also the

essence of this life—its proper pith—an insight into worldly "Shapes of delight, of mystery, and fear" is also an insight into life's spiritual repetition. The charioteer Imagination comes from heaven, peers into the mystery in human life, and returns to "the light of heaven." The mystery he sees lies in all human experience: he examines those, like the beadsman, "with upholden hand and mouth severe" and "with upward gaze"; those, like the baron and his guests, "looking back"; and those, like the lovers, who go "glad and smilingly athwart the gloom" (143-47). But the mystery is not a grisly terror to be feared; the charioteer "Looks out upon the winds with glorious fear" (128). It is an awful glory: the elfin storm into which the lovers passed was of "haggard seeming"—but a boon indeed. We might, then, have neglected the letter to Reynolds and taken our clue from "Sleep and Poetry" alone; for in it are implicit the same stages of spiritual growth that Porphyro experiences in his progress into, through, and beyond the castle of life.

Or we might equally well have depended upon the pleasure thermometer to supply the internal organizing principle of the romance. In general, the entrance into the castle and the experience in the thoughtless chamber correspond to the first two stages of the thermometer—penetration into essence by the senses and by the imagination. When we have gained this insight, "that moment have we stept / Into a sort of oneness." Porphyro, having attained that stage, is now ready for progress to Madeline's chamber, that is, for

> Richer entanglements, enthralments far
> More self-destroying, leading, by degrees,
> To the chief intensity.

At the height of these intensities is love, which absorbs

> till in the end,
> Melting into its radiance, we blend,
> Mingle, and so become a part of it.

[134]

Thus Porphyro "melted" into Madeline's dream "as the rose /
Blendeth its odour with the violet,—/ Solution sweet." When we
have been so absorbed into essence, we are partaking of the
glorious fear, the mysterious vitality that runs through all our
existence, both mortal and immortal, so that this life is to the
next as the bud is to the full-blown rose. We are in the elfin storm
outside the castle.

But in truth, although we are justified in using all these aids
to the poem so long as they are pertinent to revealing the laws that
determine its mode of existence, they are all irrelevant once we
have entered the poetic world in which these laws function. It is as
though they supply us with the grammar and vocabulary of a
foreign language; once we have assimilated them we can read for
ourselves. For " The Eve of St. Agnes " is a self-contained poetic
cosmos; it is symbolic, not allegorical. The beadsman is not to be
translated as Christian asceticism; he is that asceticism. The union
of Porphyro and Madeline does not stand for anything, but is in
itself the mystic oxymoron which is heaven. Were the poem allegorical, it would be a system of visibilia arranged into an artistic
pattern but meaningful only by translation of the visibilia into abstractions. The interrelationship of the visibilia would, then, be
extrinsic to their existence inside the poem and would be contingent
only upon the pattern of interrelationships made by their abstract
equivalences. But the statements the poem makes are implicit in
its own *données,* in the manner of symbolism; and it is irrelevant,
therefore, to distinguish the primary and secondary levels of its
meaning, for the two are coextential.

That this should be so arises necessarily from the metaphysics
that governs Keats' visions. He did not accept the world as symbolic per se; things require an ardent pursuit by man's spirit to
make them " ethereal "—symbolic. Only in man's spiritual self do
presences become essences, being in themselves only real or semi-

real things, or nothings. Man, not God, is the etherealizer, the symbolizer. And yet, a human life of sensations is itself symbolic, for such a life etherealizes itself through its own ardor and thus becomes a symbol of values. The basis of this belief is Keats' assumption that the intense experiences of life and the values which make them intelligible are different degrees of the same thing. Since " we shall enjoy ourselves here after by having what we called happiness on Earth repeated in a finer tone," and since all values reside in this spiritual repetition, then the sensations of human life are prefigurative of these values and are causally related to them. Hence the life of sensations is symbolic because it creates its own hereafter and consequently its own meaning. It is a symbol in Coleridge's sense of the term, despite the difference between the metaphysics of the two men:

> a symbol . . . is characterized by a translucence of the special in the individual, or of the general in the special, or of the universal in the general; above all by the translucence of the eternal through and in the temporal. It always partakes of the reality which it renders intelligible; and while it enunciates the whole, abides itself a living part in that unity of which it is the representative.[38]

Because of Keats' basic premise, the life of sensations cannot be other than a temporal foreshadowing of the eternal and partake of the reality which it renders intelligible. Indeed, it creates that reality, for each man's existence in eternity is a spiritual re-enactment of his temporal happiness, and intensity of experience will cause human life to partake of its own spiritual core, that essence in which all values are to be found. Therefore the climax of Porphyro's career is his etherealizing of himself through the superlative degree of his sensations (318), his self-elevation into a symbol; it is at this point that his existence has taken on a value, and is

---

[38] *The Statesman's Manual,* in *Works,* ed. Shedd, I. 437.

becoming a living part of that unity of which it is the representative.

The man of sensations, then, is the symbolizer; and, because his temporal and his eternal lives are a continuum causally connected, he is also the symbol. And what is symbolic in him is not a single deed—not, let us say, Porphyro's heaping up the fruits or yearning for Madeline—but the total pattern that his life weaves; it is this total pattern of increasing intensities that is prefigurative of the future beauty-truth in which are all ultimate values. The total career of Porphyro's existence, the abstract direction it takes, is the symbol; and that pattern, once it is clear that it is a pattern, does not require elucidation from a casual letter or any other passage in Keats' poetry, since it resides necessarily in the poem itself.

Of these presuppositions and their consequences Keats was himself acutely aware—although he used the word " allegory " in the sense in which we have used the word " symbolism ":

> . . . they are very shallow people who take every thing literally. A Man's life of any worth is a continual allegory—and very few eyes can see the Mystery of his life—a life like the scriptures, figurative—which such people can no more make out than they can the hebrew Bible. . . . Shakspeare led a life of Allegory: his works are the comments on it.[39]

No better account of the controlling principle of " The Eve of St. Agnes " is possible. The " life of any worth," it is clear, must be a life of sensations; and its mystery, of which it is figurative, is the spiritual re-enactment which it makes possible. Such a life is both itself and part of that ultimate reality it renders intelligible. What the artist does is to live this life of worth and to capture its meaning, its spiritual repetition, in his art. Art, therefore, is a mode of representing in its finer tone the life of sensations. And " The Eve of St. Agnes " is a special enactment of such a life—like Shakespeare's plays, a comment on it. *such a life ·*

---

[39] Letter to George and Georgiana Keats, February 14–May 3, 1819.

Lamia

Part I

Upon a time, before the faery broods
Drove Nymph and Satyr from the prosperous woods,
Before King Oberon's bright diadem,
Sceptre, and mantle, clasp'd with dewy gem,
Frighted away the Dryads and the Fauns
From rushes green, and brakes, and cowslip'd lawns,
The ever-smitten Hermes empty left
His golden throne, bent warm on amorous theft:
From high Olympus had he stolen light,
On this side of Jove's clouds, to escape the sight   10
Of his great summoner, and made retreat
Into a forest on the shores of Crete.
For somewhere in that sacred island dwelt
A nymph, to whom all hoofed Satyrs knelt;
At whose white feet the languid Tritons poured
Pearls, while on land they wither'd and adored.
Fast by the springs where she to bathe was wont,
And in those meads where sometime she might haunt,
Were strewn rich gifts, unknown to any Muse,
Though Fancy's casket were unlock'd to choose.   20
Ah, what a world of love was at her feet!
So Hermes thought, and a celestial heat
Burnt from his winged heels to either ear,
That from a whiteness, as the lily clear,
Blush'd into roses 'mid his golden hair,
Fallen in jealous curls about his shoulders bare.
From vale to vale, from wood to wood, he flew,
Breathing upon the flowers his passion new,
And wound with many a river to its head,
To find where this sweet nymph prepar'd her secret bed: 30
In vain; the sweet nymph might nowhere be found,
And so he rested, on the lonely ground,

Pensive, and full of painful jealousies
Of the Wood-Gods, and even the very trees.
There as he stood, he heard a mournful voice,
Such as once heard, in gentle heart, destroys
All pain but pity: thus the lone voice spake:
' When from this wreathed tomb shall I awake!
' When move in a sweet body fit for life,
' And love, and pleasure, and the ruddy strife   40
' Of hearts and lips! Ah, miserable me!'
The God, dove-footed, glided silently
Round bush and tree, soft-brushing, in his speed,
The taller grasses and full-flowering weed,
Until he found a palpitating snake,
Bright, and cirque-couchant in a dusky brake.

   She was a gordian shape of dazzling hue,
Vermilion-spotted, golden, green, and blue;
Striped like a zebra, freckled like a pard,
Eyed like a peacock, and all crimson barr'd;   50
And full of silver moons, that, as she breathed,
Dissolv'd, or brighter shone, or interwreathed
Their lustres with the gloomier tapestries—
So rainbow-sided, touch'd with miseries,
She seem'd, at once, some penanced lady elf,
Some demon's mistress, or the demon's self.
Upon her crest she wore a wannish fire
Sprinkled with stars, like Ariadne's tiar:
Her head was serpent, but ah, bitter-sweet!
She had a woman's mouth with all its pearls complete: 60
And for her eyes: what could such eyes do there
But weep, and weep, that they were born so fair?
As Proserpine still weeps for her Sicilian air.
Her throat was serpent, but the words she spake
Came, as through bubbling honey, for Love's sake,
And thus; while Hermes on his pinions lay,
Like a stoop'd falcon ere he takes his prey.

   ' Fair Hermes, crown'd with feathers, fluttering light,

' I had a splendid dream of thee last night:
' I saw thee sitting, on a throne of gold,   70
' Among the Gods, upon Olympus old,
' The only sad one; for thou didst not hear
' The soft, lute-finger'd Muses chaunting clear,
' Nor even Apollo when he sang alone,
' Deaf to his throbbing throat's long, long melodious moan.
' I dreamt I saw thee, robed in purple flakes,
' Break amorous through the clouds, as morning breaks,
' And, swiftly as a bright Phœbean dart,
' Strike for the Cretan isle; and here thou art!
' Too gentle Hermes, hast thou found the maid?'   80
Whereat the star of Lethe not delay'd
His rosy eloquence, and thus inquired:
' Thou smooth-lipp'd serpent, surely high inspired!
' Thou beauteous wreath, with melancholy eyes,
' Possess whatever bliss thou canst devise,
' Telling me only where my nymph is fled,—
' Where she doth breathe!' ' Bright planet, thou hast said,'
Return'd the snake, ' but seal with oaths, fair God!'
' I swear,' said Hermes, ' by my serpent rod,
' And by thine eyes, and by thy starry crown!'   90
Light flew his earnest words, among the blossoms blown.
Then thus again the brilliance feminine:
' Too frail of heart! for this lost nymph of thine,
' Free as the air, invisibly, she strays
' About these thornless wilds; her pleasant days
' She tastes unseen; unseen her nimble feet
' Leave traces in the grass and flowers sweet;
' From weary tendrils, and bow'd branches green,
' She plucks the fruit unseen, she bathes unseen:
' And by my power is her beauty veil'd   100
' To keep it unaffronted, unassail'd
' By the love-glances of unlovely eyes,
' Of Satyrs, Fauns, and blear'd Silenus' sighs.
' Pale grew her immortality, for woe
' Of all these lovers, and she grieved so

' I took compassion on her, bade her steep
' Her hair in weird syrops, that would keep
' Her loveliness invisible, yet free
' To wander as she loves, in liberty.
' Thou shalt behold her, Hermes, thou alone,   110
' If thou wilt, as thou swearest, grant my boon ! '
Then, once again, the charmed God began
An oath, and through the serpent's ears it ran
Warm, tremulous, devout, psalterian.
Ravish'd, she lifted her Circean head,
Blush'd a live damask, and swift-lisping said,
' I was a woman, let me have once more
' A woman's shape, and charming as before.
' I love a youth of Corinth—O the bliss !
' Give me my woman's form, and place me where he is.   120
' Stoop, Hermes, let me breathe upon thy brow,
' And thou shalt see thy sweet nymph even now.'
The God on half-shut feathers sank serene,
She breath'd upon his eyes, and swift was seen
Of both the guarded nymph near-smiling on the green.
It was no dream; or say a dream it was,
Real are the dreams of Gods, and smoothly pass
Their pleasures in a long immortal dream.
One warm, flush'd moment, hovering, it might seem
Dash'd by the wood-nymph's beauty, so he burn'd;   130
Then, lighting on the printless verdure, turn'd
To the swoon'd serpent, and with languid arm,
Delicate, put to proof the lythe Caducean charm.
So done, upon the nymph his eyes he bent
Full of adoring tears and blandishment,
And towards her stept: she, like a moon in wane,
Faded before him, cower'd, nor could restrain
Her fearful sobs, self-folding like a flower
That faints into itself at evening hour :
But the God fostering her chilled hand,   140
She felt the warmth, her eyelids open'd bland,
And, like new flowers at morning song of bees,

Bloom'd, and gave up her honey to the lees.
Into the green-recessed woods they flew;
Nor grew they pale, as mortal lovers do.

   Left to herself, the serpent now began
To change; her elfin blood in madness ran,
Her mouth foam'd, and the grass, therewith besprent,
Wither'd at dew so sweet and virulent;
Her eyes in torture fix'd, and anguish drear,   150
Hot, glaz'd, and wide, with lid-lashes all sear,
Flash'd phosphor and sharp sparks, without one cooling tear.
The colours all inflam'd throughout her train,
She writh'd about, convuls'd with scarlet pain:
A deep volcanian yellow took the place
Of all her milder-mooned body's grace;
And, as the lava ravishes the mead,
Spoilt all her silver mail, and golden brede,
Made gloom of all her frecklings, streaks and bars,
Eclips'd her crescents, and lick'd up her stars: 160
So that, in moments few, she was undrest
Of all her sapphires, greens, and amethyst,
And rubious-argent: of all these bereft,
Nothing but pain and ugliness were left.
Still shone her crown; that vanish'd, also she
Melted and disappear'd as suddenly;
And in the air, her new voice luting soft,
Cried, ' Lycius! gentle Lycius!'—Borne aloft
With the bright mists about the mountains hoar
These words dissolv'd: Crete's forests heard no more.   170

   Whither fled Lamia, now a lady bright,
A full-born beauty new and exquisite?
She fled into that valley they pass o'er
Who go to Corinth from Cenchreas' shore;
And rested at the foot of those wild hills,
The rugged founts of the Peræan rills,
And of that other ridge whose barren back
Stretches, with all its mist and cloudy rack,

South-westward to Cleone. There she stood
About a young bird's flutter from a wood,   180
Fair, on a sloping green of mossy tread,
By a clear pool, wherein she passioned
To see herself escap'd from so sore ills,
While her robes flaunted with the daffodils.

Ah, happy Lycius!—for she was a maid
More beautiful than ever twisted braid,
Or sigh'd, or blush'd, or on spring-flowered lea
Spread a green kirtle to the minstrelsy:
A virgin purest lipp'd, yet in the lore
Of love deep learned to the red heart's core: 190
Not one hour old, yet of sciential brain
To unperplex bliss from its neighbour pain;
Define their pettish limits, and estrange
Their points of contact, and swift counterchange;
Intrigue with the specious chaos, and dispart
Its most ambiguous atoms with sure art;
As though in Cupid's college she had spent
Sweet days a lovely graduate, still unshent,
And kept his rosy terms in idle languishment.

Why this fair creature chose so fairily   200
By the wayside to linger, we shall see;
But first 'tis fit to tell how she could muse
And dream, when in the serpent prison-house,
Of all she list, strange or magnificent:
How, ever, where she will'd, her spirit went;
Whether to faint Elysium, or where
Down through tress-lifting waves the Nereids fair
Wind into Thetis' bower by many a pearly stair;
Or where God Bacchus drains his cups divine,
Stretch'd out, at ease, beneath a glutinous pine;   210
Or where in Pluto's gardens palatine
Mulciber's columns gleam in far piazzian line.
And sometimes into cities she would send
Her dream, with feast and rioting to blend;

And once, while among mortals dreaming thus,
She saw the young Corinthian Lycius
Charioting foremost in the envious race,
Like a young Jove with calm uneager face,
And fell into a swooning love of him.
Now on the moth-time of that evening dim   220
He would return that way, as well she knew,
To Corinth from the shore; for freshly blew
The eastern soft wind, and his galley now
Grated the quaystones with her brazen prow
In port Cenchreas, from Egina isle
Fresh anchor'd; whither he had been awhile
To sacrifice to Jove, whose temple there
Waits with high marble doors for blood and incense rare.
Jove heard his vows, and better'd his desire;
For by some freakful chance he made retire   230
From his companions, and set forth to walk,
Perhaps grown wearied of their Corinth talk:
Over the solitary hills he fared,
Thoughtless at first, but ere eve's star appeared
His phantasy was lost, where reason fades,
In the calm'd twilight of Platonic shades.
Lamia beheld him coming, near, more near—
Close to her passing, in indifference drear,
His silent sandals swept the mossy green;
So neighbour'd to him, and yet so unseen   240
She stood: he pass'd, shut up in mysteries,
His mind wrapp'd like his mantle, while her eyes
Follow'd his steps, and her neck regal white
Turn'd—syllabling thus, ' Ah, Lycius bright,
' And will you leave me on the hills alone?
' Lycius, look back! and be some pity shown.'
He did; not with cold wonder fearingly,
But Orpheus-like at an Eurydice;
For so delicious were the words she sung,
It seem'd he had lov'd them a whole summer long: 250
And soon his eyes had drunk her beauty up,

Leaving no drop in the bewildering cup,
And still the cup was full,—while he, afraid
Lest she should vanish ere his lip had paid
Due adoration, thus began to adore;
Her soft look growing coy, she saw his chain so sure:
'Leave thee alone! Look back! Ah, Goddess, see
'Whether my eyes can ever turn from thee!
'For pity do not this sad heart belie—
'Even as thou vanishest so I shall die.   260
'Stay! though a Naiad of the rivers, stay!
'To thy far wishes will thy streams obey:
'Stay! though the greenest woods be thy domain,
'Alone they can drink up the morning rain:
'Though a descended Pleiad, will not one
'Of thine harmonious sisters keep in tune
'Thy spheres, and as thy silver proxy shine?
'So sweetly to these ravish'd ears of mine
'Came thy sweet greeting, that if thou shouldst fade
'Thy memory will waste me to a shade:—   270
'For pity do not melt!'—'If I should stay,'
Said Lamia, 'here, upon this floor of clay,
'And pain my steps upon these flowers too rough,
'What canst thou say or do of charm enough
'To dull the nice remembrance of my home?
'Thou canst not ask me with thee here to roam
'Over these hills and vales, where no joy is,—
'Empty of immortality and bliss!
'Thou art a scholar, Lycius, and must know
'That finer spirits cannot breathe below   280
'In human climes, and live: Alas! poor youth,
'What taste of purer air hast thou to soothe
'My essence? What serener palaces,
'Where I may all my many senses please,
'And by mysterious sleights a hundred thirsts appease?
'It cannot be—Adieu!' So said, she rose
Tiptoe with white arms spread. He, sick to lose
The amorous promise of her lone complain,

Swoon'd, murmuring of love, and pale with pain.
The cruel lady, without any show   290
Of sorrow for her tender favourite's woe,
But rather, if her eyes could brighter be,
With brighter eyes and slow amenity,
Put her new lips to his, and gave afresh
The life she had so tangled in her mesh:
And as he from one trance was wakening
Into another, she began to sing,
Happy in beauty, life, and love, and every thing,
A song of love, too sweet for earthly lyres,
While, like held breath, the stars drew in their panting fires.   300
And then she whisper'd in such trembling tone,
As those who, safe together met alone
For the first time through many anguish'd days,
Use other speech than looks; bidding him raise
His drooping head, and clear his soul of doubt,
For that she was a woman, and without
Any more subtle fluid in her veins
Than throbbing blood, and that the self-same pains
Inhabited her frail-strung heart as his.
And next she wonder'd how his eyes could miss   310
Her face so long in Corinth, where, she said,
She dwelt but half retir'd, and there had led
Days happy as the gold coin could invent
Without the aid of love; yet in content
Till she saw him, as once she pass'd him by,
Where 'gainst a column he leant thoughtfully
At Venus' temple porch, 'mid baskets heap'd
Of amorous herbs and flowers, newly reap'd
Late on that eve, as 'twas the night before
The Adonian feast; whereof she saw no more,   320
But wept alone those days, for why should she adore?
Lycius from death awoke into amaze,
To see her still, and singing so sweet lays;
Then from amaze into delight he fell
To hear her whisper woman's lore so well;

And every word she spake entic'd him on
To unperplex'd delight and pleasure known.
Let the mad poets say whate'er they please
Of the sweets of Fairies, Peris, Goddesses,
There is not such a treat among them all,   330
Haunters of cavern, lake, and waterfall,
As a real woman, lineal indeed
From Pyrrha's pebbles or old Adam's seed.
Thus gentle Lamia judg'd, and judg'd aright,
That Lycius could not love in half a fright,
So threw the goddess off, and won his heart
More pleasantly by playing woman's part,
With no more awe than what her beauty gave,
That, while it smote, still guaranteed to save.
Lycius to all made eloquent reply,   340
Marrying to every word a twinborn sigh;
And last, pointing to Corinth, ask'd her sweet,
If 'twas too far that night for her soft feet.
The way was short, for Lamia's eagerness
Made, by a spell, the triple league decrease
To a few paces; not at all surmised
By blinded Lycius, so in her comprized.
They pass'd the city gates, he knew not how,
So noiseless, and he never thought to know.

As men talk in a dream, so Corinth all,   350
Throughout her palaces imperial,
And all her populous streets and temples lewd,
Mutter'd, like tempest in the distance brew'd,
To the wide-spreaded night above her towers.
Men, women, rich and poor, in the cool hours,
Shuffled their sandals o'er the pavement white,
Companion'd or alone; while many a light
Flared, here and there, from wealthy festivals,
And threw their moving shadows on the walls,
Or found them cluster'd in the corniced shade   360
Of some arch'd temple door, or dusky colonnade.

Muffling his face, of greeting friends in fear,
Her fingers he press'd hard, as one came near
With curl'd gray beard, sharp eyes, and smooth bald crown,
Slow-stepp'd, and robed in philosophic gown:
Lycius shrank closer, as they met and past,
Into his mantle, adding wings to haste,
While hurried Lamia trembled: ' Ah,' said he,
' Why do you shudder, love, so ruefully?
' Why does your tender palm dissolve in dew?'—   370
' I'm wearied,' said fair Lamia: ' tell me who
' Is that old man? I cannot bring to mind
' His features:—Lycius! wherefore did you blind
' Yourself from his quick eyes?' Lycius replied,
' 'Tis Apollonius sage, my trusty guide
' And good instructor; but to-night he seems
' The ghost of folly haunting my sweet dreams.'

    While yet he spake they had arrived before
A pillar'd porch, with lofty portal door,
Where hung a silver lamp, whose phosphor glow   380
Reflected in the slabbed steps below,
Mild as a star in water; for so new,
And so unsullied was the marble hue,
So through the crystal polish, liquid fine,
Ran the dark veins, that none but feet divine
Could e'er have touch'd there. Sounds Æolian
Breath'd from the hinges, as the ample span
Of the wide doors disclos'd a place unknown
Some time to any, but those two alone,
And a few Persian mutes, who that same year   390
Were seen about the markets: none knew where
They could inhabit; the most curious
Were foil'd, who watch'd to trace them to their house:
And but the flitter-winged verse must tell
For truth's sake, what woe afterwards befel,
'Twould humour many a heart to leave them thus,
Shut from the busy world of more incredulous.

Part II

Love in a hut, with water and a crust,
Is—Love, forgive us!—cinders, ashes, dust;
Love in a palace is perhaps at last
More grievous torment than a hermit's fast:—
That is a doubtful tale from faery land,
Hard for the non-elect to understand.
Had Lycius liv'd to hand his story down,
He might have given the moral a fresh frown,
Or clench'd it quite: but too short was their bliss
To breed distrust and hate, that make the soft voice hiss.   10
Besides, there, nightly, with terrific glare,
Love, jealous grown of so complete a pair,
Hover'd and buzz'd his wings, with fearful roar,
Above the lintel of their chamber door,
And down the passage cast a glow upon the floor.

   For all this came a ruin: side by side
They were enthroned, in the even tide,
Upon a couch, near to a curtaining
Whose airy texture, from a golden string,
Floated into the room, and let appear   20
Unveil'd the summer heaven, blue and clear,
Betwixt two marble shafts:—there they reposed,
Where use had made it sweet, with eyelids closed,
Saving a tythe which love still open kept,
That they might see each other while they almost slept;
When from the slope side of a suburb hill,
Deafening the swallow's twitter, came a thrill
Of trumpets—Lycius started—the sounds fled,
But left a thought a-buzzing in his head.
For the first time, since first he harbour'd in   30
That purple-lined palace of sweet sin,
His spirit pass'd beyond its golden bourn
Into the noisy world almost forsworn.
The lady, ever watchful, penetrant,
Saw this with pain, so arguing a want

Of something more, more than her empery
Of joys; and she began to moan and sigh
Because he mused beyond her, knowing well
That but a moment's thought is passion's passing bell.
'Why do you sigh, fair creature?' whisper'd he: 40
'Why do you think?' return'd she tenderly:
'You have deserted me;—where am I now?
'Not in your heart while care weighs on your brow:
'No, no, you have dismiss'd me; and I go
'From your breast houseless: ay, it must be so.'
He answer'd, bending to her open eyes,
Where he was mirror'd small in paradise,
'My silver planet, both of eve and morn!
'Why will you plead yourself so sad forlorn,
'While I am striving how to fill my heart   50
'With deeper crimson, and a double smart?
'How to entangle, trammel up and snare
'Your soul in mine, and labyrinth you there
'Like the hid scent in an unbudded rose?
'Ay, a sweet kiss—you see your mighty woes.
'My thoughts! shall I unveil them? Listen then!
'What mortal hath a prize, that other men
'May be confounded and abash'd withal,
'But lets it sometimes pace abroad majestical,
'And triumph, as in thee I should rejoice   60
'Amid the hoarse alarm of Corinth's voice.
'Let my foes choke, and my friends shout afar,
'While through the thronged streets your bridal car
'Wheels round its dazzling spokes.'—The lady's cheek
Trembled; she nothing said, but, pale and meek,
Arose and knelt before him, wept a rain
Of sorrows at his words; at last with pain
Beseeching him, the while his hand she wrung,
To change his purpose. He thereat was stung,
Perverse, with stronger fancy to reclaim   70
Her wild and timid nature to his aim:
Besides, for all his love, in self despite

Against his better self, he took delight
Luxurious in her sorrows, soft and new.
His passion, cruel grown, took on a hue
Fierce and sanguineous as 'twas possible
In one whose brow had no dark veins to swell.
Fine was the mitigated fury, like
Apollo's presence when in act to strike
The serpent—Ha, the serpent! certes, she   80
Was none. She burnt, she lov'd the tyranny,
And, all subdued, consented to the hour
When to the bridal he should lead his paramour.
Whispering in midnight silence, said the youth,
' Sure some sweet name thou hast, though, by my truth,
' I have not ask'd it, ever thinking thee
' Not mortal, but of heavenly progeny,
' As still I do. Hast any mortal name,
' Fit appellation for this dazzling frame?
' Or friends or kinsfolk on the citied earth,   90
' To share our marriage feast and nuptial mirth?'
' I have no friends,' said Lamia, ' no, not one;
' My presence in wide Corinth hardly known:
' My parents' bones are in their dusty urns
' Sepulchred, where no kindled incense burns,
' Seeing all their luckless race are dead, save me,
' And I neglect the holy rite for thee.
' Even as you list invite your many guests;
' But if, as now it seems, your vision rests
' With any pleasure on me, do not bid   100
' Old Apollonius—from him keep me hid.'
Lycius, perplex'd at words so blind and blank,
Made close inquiry; from whose touch she shrank,
Feigning a sleep; and he to the dull shade
Of deep sleep in a moment was betray'd.

It was the custom then to bring away
The bride from home at blushing shut of day,
Veil'd, in a chariot, heralded along

By strewn flowers, torches, and a marriage song,
With other pageants: but this fair unknown   110
Had not a friend. So being left alone,
(Lycius was gone to summon all his kin)
And knowing surely she could never win
His foolish heart from its mad pompousness,
She set herself, high-thoughted, how to dress
The misery in fit magnificence.
She did so, but 'tis doubtful how and whence
Came, and who were her subtle servitors.
About the halls, and to and from the doors,
There was a noise of wings, till in short space   120
The glowing banquet-room shone with wide-arched grace.
A haunting music, sole perhaps and lone
Supportress of the faery-roof, made moan
Throughout, as fearful the whole charm might fade.
Fresh carved cedar, mimicking a glade
Of palm and plantain, met from either side,
High in the midst, in honour of the bride:
Two palms and then two plantains, and so on,
From either side their stems branch'd one to one
All down the aisled place; and beneath all   130
There ran a stream of lamps straight on from wall to wall.
So canopied, lay an untasted feast
Teeming with odours. Lamia, regal drest,
Silently paced about, and as she went,
In pale contented sort of discontent,
Mission'd her viewless servants to enrich
The fretted splendour of each nook and niche.
Between the tree-stems, marbled plain at first,
Came jasper pannels; then, anon, there burst
Forth creeping imagery of slighter trees,   140
And with the larger wove in small intricacies.
Approving all, she faded at self-will,
And shut the chamber up, close, hush'd and still.
Complete and ready for the revels rude,
When dreadful guests would come to spoil her solitude.

The day appear'd, and all the gossip rout.
O senseless Lycius! Madman! wherefore flout
The silent-blessing fate, warm cloister'd hours,
And show to common eyes these secret bowers?
The herd approach'd; each guest, with busy brain,   150
Arriving at the portal, gaz'd amain,
And enter'd marveling: for they knew the street,
Remember'd it from childhood all complete
Without a gap, yet ne'er before had seen
That royal porch, that high-built fair demesne;
So in they hurried all, maz'd, curious and keen:
Save one, who look'd thereon with eye severe,
And with calm-planted steps walk'd in austere;
'Twas Apollonius: something too he laugh'd,
As though some knotty problem, that had daft   160
His patient thought, had now begun to thaw,
And solve and melt:—'twas just as he foresaw.

He met within the murmurous vestibule
His young disciple. ' 'Tis no common rule,
' Lycius,' said he, ' for uninvited guest
' To force himself upon you, and infest
' With an unbidden presence the bright throng
' Of younger friends; yet must I do this wrong,
' And you forgive me.' Lycius blush'd, and led
The old man through the inner doors broad-spread;   170
With reconciling words and courteous mien
Turning into sweet milk the sophist's spleen.

Of wealthy lustre was the banquet-room,
Fill'd with pervading brilliance and perfume:
Before each lucid pannel fuming stood
A censer fed with myrrh and spiced wood,
Each by a sacred tripod held aloft,
Whose slender feet wide-swerv'd upon the soft
Wool-woofed carpets: fifty wreaths of smoke
From fifty censers their light voyage took   180
To the high roof, still mimick'd as they rose

Along the mirror'd walls by twin-clouds odorous.
Twelve sphered tables, by silk seats insphered,
High as the level of a man's breast rear'd
On libbard's paws, upheld the heavy gold
Of cups and goblets, and the store thrice told
Of Ceres' horn, and, in huge vessels, wine
Come from the gloomy tun with merry shine.
Thus loaded with a feast the tables stood,
Each shrining in the midst the image of a God.   190

   When in an antichamber every guest
Had felt the cold full sponge to pleasure press'd,
By minist'ring slaves, upon his hands and feet,
And fragrant oils with ceremony meet
Pour'd on his hair, they all mov'd to the feast
In white robes, and themselves in order placed
Around the silken couches, wondering
Whence all this mighty cost and blaze of wealth could spring.

   Soft went the music the soft air along,
While fluent Greek a vowel'd undersong   200
Kept up among the guests, discoursing low
At first, for scarcely was the wine at flow;
But when the happy vintage touch'd their brains,
Louder they talk, and louder come the strains
Of powerful instruments:—the gorgeous dyes,
The space, the splendour of the draperies,
The roof of awful richness, nectarous cheer,
Beautiful slaves, and Lamia's self, appear,
Now, when the wine has done its rosy deed,
And every soul from human trammels freed,   210
No more so strange; for merry wine, sweet wine,
Will make Elysian shades not too fair, too divine.
Soon was God Bacchus at meridian height;
Flush'd were their cheeks, and bright eyes double bright:
Garlands of every green, and every scent
From vales deflower'd, or forest-trees branch-rent,
In baskets of bright osier'd gold were brought

High as the handles heap'd, to suit the thought
Of every guest; that each, as he did please,
Might fancy-fit his brows, silk-pillow'd at his ease.   220

What wreath for Lamia? What for Lycius?
What for the sage, old Apollonius?
Upon her aching forehead be there hung
The leaves of willow and of adder's tongue;
And for the youth, quick, let us strip for him
The thyrsus, that his watching eyes may swim
Into forgetfulness; and, for the sage,
Let spear-grass and the spiteful thistle wage
War on his temples. Do not all charms fly
At the mere touch of cold philosophy?   230
There was an awful rainbow once in heaven:
We know her woof, her texture; she is given
In the dull catalogue of common things.
Philosophy will clip an Angel's wings,
Conquer all mysteries by rule and line,
Empty the haunted air, and gnomed mine—
Unweave a rainbow, as it erewhile made
The tender-person'd Lamia melt into a shade.

By her glad Lycius sitting, in chief place,
Scarce saw in all the room another face,   240
Till, checking his love trance, a cup he took
Full brimm'd, and opposite sent forth a look
'Cross the broad table, to beseech a glance
From his old teacher's wrinkled countenance,
And pledge him. The bald-head philosopher
Had fix'd his eye, without a twinkle or stir
Full on the alarmed beauty of the bride,
Brow-beating her fair form, and troubling her sweet pride.
Lycius then press'd her hand, with devout touch,
As pale it lay upon the rosy couch: 250
'Twas icy, and the cold ran through his veins;
Then sudden it grew hot, and all the pains
Of an unnatural heat shot to his heart.

'Lamia, what means this? Wherefore dost thou start?
'Know'st thou that man?' Poor Lamia answer'd not.
He gaz'd into her eyes, and not a jot
Own'd they the lovelorn piteous appeal:
More, more he gaz'd: his human senses reel:
Some hungry spell that loveliness absorbs;
There was no recognition in those orbs.   260
'Lamia!' he cried—and no soft-toned reply.
The many heard, and the loud revelry
Grew hush; the stately music no more breathes;
The myrtle sicken'd in a thousand wreaths.
By faint degrees, voice, lute, and pleasure ceased;
A deadly silence step by step increased,
Until it seem'd a horrid presence there,
And not a man but felt the terror in his hair.
'Lamia!' he shriek'd; and nothing but the shriek
With its sad echo did the silence break.   270
'Begone, foul dream!' he cried, gazing again
In the bride's face, where now no azure vein
Wander'd on fair-spaced temples; no soft bloom
Misted the cheek; no passion to illume
The deep-recessed vision:—all was blight;
Lamia, no longer fair, there sat a deadly white.
'Shut, shut those juggling eyes, thou ruthless man!
'Turn them aside, wretch! or the righteous ban
'Of all the Gods, whose dreadful images
'Here represent their shadowy presences,   280
'May pierce them on the sudden with the thorn
'Of painful blindness; leaving thee forlorn,
'In trembling dotage to the feeblest fright
'Of conscience, for their long offended might,
'For all thine impious proud-heart sophistries,
'Unlawful magic, and enticing lies.
'Corinthians! look upon that gray-beard wretch!
'Mark how, possess'd, his lashless eyelids stretch
'Around his demon eyes! Corinthians, see!
'My sweet bride withers at their potency.'   290

[156]

'Fool!' said the sophist, in an under-tone
Gruff with contempt; which a death-nighing moan
From Lycius answer'd, as heart-struck and lost,
He sank supine beside the aching ghost.
'Fool! Fool!' repeated he, while his eyes still
Relented not, nor mov'd; 'from every ill
'Of life have I preserv'd thee to this day,
'And shall I see thee made a serpent's prey?'
Then Lamia breath'd death breath; the sophist's eye,
Like a sharp spear, went through her utterly,   300
Keen, cruel, perceant, stinging; she, as well
As her weak hand could any meaning tell,
Motion'd him to be silent; vainly so,
He look'd and look'd again a level—No!
'A Serpent!' echoed he; no sooner said,
Than with a frightful scream she vanished:
And Lycius' arms were empty of delight,
As were his limbs of life, from that same night.
On the high couch he lay!—his friends came round—
Supported him—no pulse, or breath they found,   310
And, in its marriage robe, the heavy body wound.

Lamia

i

J N THE THREE poems we have been considering, Keats succeeded in unfolding his total theme by means of a single dramatic
action, even though that theme is two-fold. The ascent to the
conditions of heaven and then the inevitable journey homeward to
habitual self are a continuous dramatic movement in the " Ode on
a Grecian Urn " and " La Belle Dame Sans Merci ": statement
leads organically to counterstatement. Indeed, in the ode statement
and counterstatement are so integrated as to resolve each other in a
synthesis. In " The Eve of St. Agnes " the dramatic form is
equally organic, for the counterstatements to the lovers' triumphant
access to the mystery are perfectly blended in as either functionally
subordinate actors or as a dramatically contrasting frame that
gives depth to the central theme.

In " Lamia," however, Keats has chosen to convey his theme
by means of a contrast between union with essence under the
conditions of the ideal world and union with essence in the world
of mutability. The consequence of his choice of artistry is a dis-
junction of the dramatic components: Hermes and the nymph
on the one hand, and Lycius and Lamia on the other, form two
independent narratives, and the presence of Lamia in both is
hardly a sufficient cohesive force to cause the two themes to
play upon each other in the reader's mind. Once Lamia has been
granted her wish to return to human form, Hermes and the
nymph are irrelevant to the subsequent action; nor do they even

linger as an ironic backdrop against which Lycius and Lamia act out the tragedy of human yearning for an immortality of passion.

ii

Despite the failure of the poem as a thematic narrative, the story of Hermes and the nymph gives to the subsequent narrative its point, although not a depth. It helps make clear the experiences of Lycius and Lamia, but, because Keats failed to integrate it with the events it introduces, it does not come into focus with that meaning to give it the necessary stereoscopic dimensions.

The nymph whom Hermes seeks resembles Madeline in many ways and has approximately the same symbolic values. Being ideal beauty, a kind of Cynthia, she must be loved as that ideal, and not merely as sensuous loveliness. Only those weak in spirit, like Angela, understand love to be the " mere commingling of passionate breath." But the fauns, hoofed satyrs, and sileni—the sensual followers of Bacchus and Pan—look upon the nymph only with the gross senses and fail to recognize the essence of beauty that lies within the outer form. They look on her only with " the love-glances of unlovely eyes " (I. 102) and woo her with things of rich material beauty. Thus " for woe / Of all these lovers " " Pale grew her immortality " (I. 104-105)—just as the immortal Porphyro grew pale in Madeline's vision and moved towards mortality when his earthly form intruded; and the nymph becomes grieved—just as Madeline was frightened by the gross physical reality. Therefore, the nymph has been made invisible, for ideal beauty is beyond the senses and can be perceived only by a supernal magic. Only by an ascent through the chambers of life could Porphyro enter the sweet purgatory to look on naked beauty in the paradise beyond; access to the silent sphery sessions held by the powers in water, fiery realm, and airy bourne can be gained only " by a patient wing, a constant spell, / Or by ethereal things."

Having been placed, like the " unheard " melodies, beyond the senses so as not to be desecrated by them, the nymph is free as the air and strays invisibly in all places, to be found everywhere and yet inaccessible to ordinary sense.

To Hermes alone will she be known, for Hermes, although " Too frail of heart," now burns with " a celestial heat " (I. 22). Like Porphyro, he has attained a passionate intensity which, when a miracle unveils the ideal nymph to him, allows the chaste ideal and the transcendently passionate to coalesce and become an eternal love. But Lamia's miracle does not make the nymph visible to all; only in Hermes' visions is she perceptible: " Thou shalt behold her, Hermes, thou alone " (I. 110). She is visible, not because she is made physical, but because Hermes gains the power to perceive her presence: she is now a " known Unknown." This sensual-spiritual opposition of the sileni and Hermes was a fixed symbolic pattern in Keats' mind: " Other wines of a heavy and spirituous nature transform a Man to a Silenus; this [claret] makes him a Hermes." [1] Hermes' vision of the nymph is an inward experience, and each man attains it only within himself. Porphyro, too, could see the disrobing Madeline only from the privacy of the closet, for it is a spiritual experience of the isolated self.

Being ideal beauty, the nymph is also that Cynthia who is the completed form of all completeness; belonging to Being, this chaste immortality, whose hands are " chilled " (compare: " Cold Pastoral "), is self-contained, perfect, in need of nothing beyond itself for its own fulfillment. Consequently, upon the first approach of Hermes, the nymph—" like a moon in wane " (I. 136)—retreats into her perfect self, " self-folding like a flower / That faints into itself at evening hour " (I. 138-39), just as the sleeping Madeline is a self-contained perfection " As though a rose should shut, and be a bud again." It is the " celestial heat " (I. 22), the " warmth "

---

[1] Letter to George and Georgiana Keats, February 14–May 3, 1819.

(I. 141) of Hermes, his being beyond a mortal man impassioned far, that makes the perfection of form available to him so that the nymph " gave up her honey to the lees " (I. 143).

All the necessary conditions have now been fulfilled for an immortality of passion: in his own self Hermes has magically gained sight of the chastely ideal beauty (he has been in the Thoughtless Chamber and has advanced to the purgatorial closet adjacent to paradise) ; and he has mounted to the passionate intensity necessary in order that the ideal be available to him (he has entered the Chamber of Maiden-Thought). Now at last Hermes and the nymph may melt " as the rose / Blendeth its odour with the violet,—/ Solution sweet."

But the premise upon which Keats has constructed this myth of a perfectly attained heaven where love is forever warm is that Hermes is a god, not a mortal, just as the premise that allows Porphyro and Madeline to enter the mystery of the storm is that the occasion is St. Agnes' Eve, when mortal dreams do become truth. Man may have his ideal visions, but, lacking the miracle, he awakens into the mortal world and finds they are not truth: the elfin grot is discovered to be only a cold hill side. Only because he is a god can Hermes awaken from his dream and find it truth; or rather, there is no awakening from this dream because

> *Real are the dreams of Gods, and smoothly pass*
> *Their pleasures in a long immortal dream.* (I. 127-28)

Mortal man can only glimpse the ideal in visions and then return to reality to find that earthly beauty cannot keep her lustrous eyes. At best, he can know that the beauty he envisions will hereafter be truth, that " Imagination and its empyreal reflection is the same as human Life and its Spiritual repetition." For gods, however, the vision of ideal beauty is a reality: in heaven's bourne beauty is truth. And therefore, since Hermes and the nymph exist in the oxymoronic mystery which is the source and core of mortal life,

Into the green-recessed woods they flew;
Nor grew they pale, as mortal lovers do. (I. 144-45)

These recessed woods are the elfin storm into which Madeline and
Porphyro fled, and the shadows numberless in which the nightingale sings, and the elfin grot into which the knight-at-arms is transported. They are the mystery beyond human vision, the darkness
outside the castle of life, into which one could enter if he could
overcome the growing pale that is inherent in mortality—that is to
say, if, like Hermes, he were immortal and hence could experience
beauty as truth, dream as reality.

Here, then, is Keats' hypothesis of perfection, an ideal against
which he may examine and understand the life of mortal man.
Endymion had been a wishful adolescent illusion: immortal perfection embraces a mortal—the king's daughter marries the beggar.
" The Eve of St. Agnes " and the myth of Hermes and the nymph
are the mature " Guesses at Heaven "; [2] here Keats is not vicari-
ously fulfilling his yearnings through poetic realization, but is
speculating on perfection by presupposing that the conditions of
mortal life have been abrogated. But " La Belle Dame Sans
Merci " and the story of Lycius and Lamia are the ideal experiences of Hermes and the nymph, or of Porphyro and Madeline,
translated into human terms; and it is Keats' intention, although
he realizes it imperfectly, to sharpen the outlines of Lycius' tragedy
by painting it against a background of precisely the same events
experienced under immortal, and therefore perfect, conditions.
Lycius' dream is not real; the green-recessed woods into which
the mortal lovers flee is an illusion, and they do grow pale.

---

[2]   *Fanatics have their dreams, wherewith they weave*
        A paradise for a sect; the savage too
        From forth the loftiest fashion of his sleep
        Guesses at Heaven.
                              —The Fall of Hyperion, I. 1-4.

I underscore heavily this relation of the two narratives because I believe this is the only antithesis developed in the poem. Most examinations of the poem have centered on the relation of Lamia and Apollonius, and therefore have searched for the relation of the values they appear to represent, as though Keats were defending sensuous beauty against philosophy, or philosophy against sensuous beauty. The repeated failure to find any solution to this problem results, I believe, from the fact that there is no problem. Rather, the legend of Lycius and Lamia is an account of what needs must happen to mortal man's aspirations, not an evaluation of what inspires and destroys them, any more than " La Belle Dame Sans Merci " implies an evaluation of the lady without tenderness and the death-pale mortals who call the knight back to the cold hill side. To expect Keats to urge the sensuous life or the philosophic life is to expect of him the kind of poetry that he explicitly scorned: " We hate poetry that has a palpable design upon us." [3] He writes of his guesses at heaven and of his perceptions of life; but he does not argue a thesis. At most, his poetry is descriptive and suppositive, not prescriptive. He will examine the consequences of an hypothesis—let us say, the consequences of the beadsman's aspiring to a spiritual existence by avoiding the life of sensations; but he will not have a palpable design on us by causing his poetry to prescribe one mode of existence rather than another. For Keats is poet enough to know that poetry affirms nothing: the poetical character " does no harm from its relish of the dark side of things any more than from its taste for the bright one; because they both end in speculation." [4]

We shall examine the relation of Lamia and Apollonius more fully, but in order to do so it is necessary to recognize that the shaping principle of the poem is not this relationship but the fact

[3] Letter to Reynolds, February 3, 1818.
[4] Letter to Woodhouse, October 27, 1818.

that the legend of Hermes and the nymph and the legend of Lamia and Lycius are explorations of the same system of symbols as it functions under two different conditions, the immortal and the mortal. The first is a guess at heaven, the second is the perceptible reality seen from the perspective of that guess. Were it to perform its function perfectly—as it does not—the story of Hermes should impel a reading of the main narrative in the light of the " vast idea " that ever rolled before the poet—the vast idea that is realized fully by the immortals alone, and by mortal man only in fleeting moments.

iii

The meeting of Lamia and Lycius takes place after a set of preparations that bears some analogy to Porphyro's passage through the chambers of life before he enters Madeline's room. Lycius has been sacrificing in the temple of Jove and apparently has been requesting the fulfillment of his earthly aspirations, for " Jove heard his vows, and better'd his desire " (I. 229). Presumably Jove heightens the aspirations of Lycius' spirit, and the subsequent events are the consequences of the god's heeding the mortal's prayer. Jove's aid takes the form of separating Lycius from his companions, divorcing him from the world of men, since, like Hermes, he must see his vision of perfect beauty in the privacy of his self. Pan is " the unimaginable lodge / For *solitary* thinkings." " Thoughtless at first " (I. 234), like Porphyro in the Thoughtless Chamber, Lycius then strays beyond the confines of the conceptual mind, which can weigh only the things and relationships of the mortal world:

> *His phantasy was lost, where reason fades,*
> *In the calm'd twilight of Platonic shades.* (I. 235-36)

His mind has dodged conception on its way to the bourne of heaven, for

> *no great minist'ring reason sorts*
> *Out the dark mysteries of human souls*
> *To clear conceiving.*[5]

And because he has passed the confines of reason, he is " shut up in mysteries " (I. 241). The immortal Hermes exists in the mystery; dream is reality, beauty is truth. But for mortals, Pan, by being

> *the unimaginable lodge*
> *For solitary thinkings; such as dodge*
> *Conception to the very bourne of heaven,*

is therefore

> *Dread opener of the mysterious doors*
> *Leading to universal knowledge.*

Lycius, then, has been divinely prepared for the meeting with Lamia. Beyond the limits of the conceptual, his solitary thinkings having carried him into the mysteries, he is ready for an involvement in a vision of perfect beauty which should, ideally, form for him the conditions of heaven's bourne.

I am forced to confess that I cannot fathom the full significance of Lamia's origin or of her terribly splendid transformation into a beautiful woman. Nor do I understand why it is she who governs the visibility of the nymph, and yet requires the aid of Hermes to become metamorphosed into a woman. It is clear, however, that she is related to the " glorious fear " that pervades the charioteer Imagination in his search into the mystery; to the elfin storm which is " of haggard seeming, but a boon indeed "; to the beautiful lady without tenderness who entices the knight-at-arms. Indeed, Lamia is explicitly described as a " cruel lady, without any show / Of sorrow for her tender favourite's woe " (I. 290–91); and, like Cynthia, who " tortured " Endymion " with renewed life," [6] Lamia

---

[5] " Sleep and Poetry," 288-90.   [6] *Endymion,* I. 919.

put her lips to Lycius' and "gave afresh / The life she had so tangled in her mesh" (I. 294–95). Her beauty, "while it smote, still guaranteed to save" (I. 339) ; and thus she is related to that ideal for which mortal man agonizes and on which his immortality depends.

Beneath all these descriptions of Lamia there lurks the nature of Cynthia, and in some vague fashion Lamia is a kind of earthly version of Cynthia. Like the Cynthia of classical myth, she is the guardian of the nymph and preserves her chaste immortality against the sensuous. In her serpent form she bears Cynthia's emblems: her body is "full of silver moons" (I. 51) and Cynthia's "crescents" (I. 160) ; her crest is "Sprinkled with stars" (I. 58), it is a "starry crown" (I. 90) ; her body is "milder-mooned" (I. 156) and covered with "silver mail" (I. 158). To Lycius she seems "a descended Pleiad" (I. 265), his "silver planet, both of eve and morn" (II. 48) ; and Keats originally wrote of her "silver appellation" and her walking "silverly."

But she is not a Cynthia as Madeline is. Rather, she is as Cynthia-like as Cynthia can be in the mortal world, for here beauty and ugliness, pleasure and pain, are inseparable. And the lamia with whom the poem begins is that dualism, a beauty of the world, a Cynthia-serpent:

> *Her head was serpent, but ah, bitter-sweet!*
> *She had a woman's mouth with all its pearls complete:*
> *And for her eyes: what could such eyes do there*
> *But weep, and weep, that they were born so fair?*
> (I. 59–62)

She is both beauty and ugliness, both goddess and mortal. The miracle of her metamorphosis is that from the beauty-ugliness, which characterizes all earthly beauty, the pain and ugliness are magically wiped away: the serpent vanishes and the beauty of her womanliness is fulfilled. She is, then, beauty made palpable in such a fashion that it is freed of all the ugliness that attends such beauty in the physical world—" a maid / More beautiful than ever twisted braid " (I. 185–86) ; and her being revealed to Lycius in this form is parallel to the nymph's being made visible to Hermes. The beauty that Lamia represents, moreover, is not the sensuous beauty of the world, for her transformation is an extrication of pure beauty from the beauty-horror of the earthly; and for Lycius she is a condition that does not exist in the mutable world, since she can " unperplex bliss from its neighbour pain " (I. 192), and since she entices him to " unperplex'd delight " (I. 327). She can, that is, create for him the condition that exists only in heaven's bourne, exactly as she herself is an unearthly beauty free from its attendant earthly ugliness. Until she throws " the goddess off " (I. 336), she is as much a Cynthia to the mortal Lycius as the nymph is a Cynthia to the immortal Hermes, the difference being that pure beauty is available to the gods, but for man the vision of perfect beauty must be extracted from the ugliness that accompanies it in the world. This is not, however, to imply an evaluation of Lamia; man cannot otherwise envision the ideal.

Because Lamia is a vision of ideal beauty to Lycius, he is absorbed by her from the moment they meet. His eyes cannot ever turn from her (I. 258), even as the knight-at-arms saw nothing else but the fairy's child; and Lycius foresees that should she vanish he would die (I. 260), for in being caught up in the essence of the ideal he is truly alive, and return to his mortal self is truly a dying. Self-destroyed by her ideal beauty, he has melted into her radiance and reached that height where " Life's self is nourish'd by its proper pith ": Lamia

> Put her new lips to his, and gave afresh
> The life she had so tangled in her mesh.   (I. 294–95)

Being absorbed into Lamia's beauty, now that her Cynthia-self is disengaged from the serpent form, Lycius is led by her towards the magic palace, whose nature is reminiscent of that of the elfin grot. It is a place unknown to any but the lovers (I. 388-89); and in a sense it exists only in the spirit of Lycius, for later the wedding guests discover it to be in a space where there has been no space and hence it is as much outside the spatial as the elfin grot and the scene on the urn's frieze. Just as the nymph is revealed to Hermes alone, so the palace is initially made known and available only to Lycius.

First, however, the lovers must pass through the self-contained world where, as in the central hall of the baron's castle, life is its own end. This is the world of " populous streets and temples lewd " (I. 352), of " wealthy festivals " (I. 358)—the world of Corinth, notorious for its sensuality and corruption. And then, too, Lycius must, quite literally, dodge conception before he may approach the bourne of heaven that the magic palace symbolizes. Apollonius is not an independent value, but an inherent faculty of the mortal Lycius. The philosopher has been his " trusty guide " and " good instructor " (I. 375–76); he has preserved Lycius " from every ill / Of *life* " (II. 296–97). He is, in other words, Lycius' own conceptual brain, which is adequate to his mortal existence but is the dull brain that perplexes and retards visionary flights heavenward. In the presence of such a vision, the conceptual mind seems to Lycius the " ghost of folly haunting my sweet dreams " (I. 377). Man must be teased out of thought if he is to contemplate his home ethereal; and therefore Lycius muffles his face, shrinks into his mantle, and hastens past in order to avoid an encounter on the street with Apollonius (I. 362–67), who, although unknown to Lamia because he is unrelated to her order of being, makes her shudder at the sight of his " quick eyes " (I. 374). Having moved through the world of noisy revelry and having dodged the rational, the lovers may now enter the visionary palace,

where they are shut from the " busy world of more incredulous "
(I. 397), the world that is skeptical of guesses at heaven.

iv

The destruction of the vision comes as quickly for the mortal
Lycius as it does for the knight-at-arms: " For all this came a
ruin " (II. 16). The point is that earthly man may make his
journeys heavenward, but so long as he is mortal his " body is
earthward pressed." [7] Keats sees for man only two alternatives,
neither of them satisfactory; for to expect a heaven on earth is to
deny that life is a progress towards heaven through increasing
intensities which are both pleasure and pain. One may create his
splendid vision of beauty-truth, his Lamia's palace, but since it must
end only in the journey homeward to habitual self, it is " perhaps
at last / More grievous torment than a hermit's fast " (II. 3-4).
Or one may avoid such visions of love in the magic palace of
heaven's bourne and confine himself to the cold and impoverished
realities of the world, whose nature is not perfectible. But the
world has nothing to offer: this

> *Love in a hut, with water and a crust,*
> *Is—Love, forgive us!—cinders, ashes, dust.* (II. 1–2)

What Keats yearns for is an escape into the green-recessed woods
where one does not grow pale as mortal lovers do; but in this world
there is only the choice between the hut which is empty of spiritual
values and sensuous splendor, and the visionary palace which tor-
ments the earth-bound spirit. And yet, this truth can be known
only to the elect, those who have made the journey heavenward
(II. 5–6).

To recognize the proper significance of Lamia and Apollonius,
it is necessary to observe that Lycius alone is the cause of his

---

[7] " God of the Meridian," 4.

tragedy and that Apollonius completes the destruction only *after*
Lycius has undermined the foundation of his own visionary existence. All goes well in the palace until Lycius hears the trumpet-
sound of the noisy world. The origin of the tragedy is the necessary
weakness inherent in Lycius, as it is inherent in all mortals; and
from this weakness alone all the subsequent tragedy follows. The
trumpet call " from the slope side of a suburb hill " (II. 26) is the
" stings / Of human neighbourhood " that " envenom all "; [8] it is
the recollection of human passions that calls the poet from the
frieze to the dimensional world; it is the whisperings of the death-
pale kings and princes who warn against enthrallment in visionary
beauty and call the dreamer back to the cold hill side; it is the
recollection of his isolation from men that, like a bell, tolls the poet
back to his sole self; it is the boisterous, festive clarion, the kettle-
drum, and the clarionet in the halls of revelry that threaten to
destroy Madeline's dream-vision. It is, in short, the tug of mortality that draws man out of his visions of a beauty that is truth, a
bliss that is unperplexed from pain.

Neither Lamia nor Apollonius is responsible for this summons
from the world, nor indeed, being mortal, can Lycius avoid heeding
it; and yet that " moment's thought is passion's passing bell "
(II. 39). In the palace he had " *almost* forsworn " the noisy world
(II. 33), but so long as he remains a mortal he cannot wholly
sever the bond with humanity or shatter the fragile bar that keeps
him from his home ethereal. In the palace Lycius has made his
journey heavenward, and his spirit has passed beyond " its golden
bourn " (II. 32) ; but the trumpet call is the intrusion of the world
of humanity that now draws him out of the vision. The result is
that Lycius returns to his proper self, and the relation of Lamia
and Lycius changes correspondingly. He had been ensnared by her
ideal beauty selflessly, but now he becomes a mortal lover and

[8] *Endymion*, I. 621-22.

inverts the empathic relationship: he strives to "entangle, trammel up and snare" her soul in his (II. 52–53) instead of yielding up his own self in essence. His passion has become the mixed love-hate of mortal lovers that corresponds to the pleasure-pain of the mortal world:

> he took delight
> *Luxurious in her sorrows, soft and new.*
> *His passion, cruel grown, took on a hue*
> *Fierce and sanguineous.* (II. 73–76)

Moreover, Lamia has thrown the goddess off, to play again mortal woman's part. No longer is she Lycius' vision of a Cynthia, an ideal beauty made manifest to a mortal by extraction from beauty-horror; to Lycius she has become a real woman, "lineal indeed" (I. 332), and her taking on a merely mortal form to Lycius is manifest in her new mixed character: she is both wild and timid (II. 71). Thus, instead of capturing Lycius' spirit in hers, she yields, womanly: "She burnt, she lov'd the tyranny" (II. 81). In consequence, the love has become a worldly one, and Lycius, having been summoned back to mortality, thinks only in terms of the world. Love is a prize, not an intensity that leads to essence, and so it must be trumpeted to mortal man; it is a triumph that plays to the petty passions of hate and pride, the passions of the mortal world: "Let my foes choke, and my friends shout afar" (II. 62), cries Lycius, once he is summoned back to his mean mortal self. He is now governed, as Lamia recognizes, by a "mad pompousness" (II. 114), a sense of self-importance and a desire for display that are the opposites of the loss of self necessary for fellowship with essence. But again Keats intends no evaluation: Lycius and Lamia are neither right nor wrong. Lycius is only following the dictates of his nature, which has been recalled to the world, and there is nothing that Lamia can do but attempt to make the most of it. Man may attend the sphery sessions, but the "powers" do not call out to him or grant him special immunities.

At this stage the union of Lycius and Lamia is only a mockery of the union of Hermes and the nymph, and correspondingly the palace becomes a mockery of the green-recessed woods into which the immortals fled. It is not the dark and hidden mystery, spaceless and timeless, but a factitious simulation of the mystery because it is being prepared for view by men without dream-visions: the hall is fitted out with " Fresh carved cedar, mimicking a glade / Of palm and plantain " (II. 125–26), for the union is to be humanized and the world of rude Corinthian revelers is to be admitted into what has been the mystery. It is the inescapable call of the world that has impelled Lycius to display his triumph and make his vision available to conception; and thus he alone is responsible for the fact that the stings of human neighborhood will envenom all. The " dreadful guests " (II. 145), the " herd," being incapable of visions and as carnal as their Corinthianism implies, expect only " revels rude " (II. 144). They had never seen the palace and could scarce believe its existence. Lulled by sensuous pleasures and drunk with wine, they do not even realize they are in the presence of the mystery:

> for merry wine, sweet wine,
> Will make Elysian shades not too fair, too divine.
> (II. 211–12)

The Corinthians, therefore, correspond to the satyrs and sileni who make pale the immortality of the nymph; like those other followers of Bacchus, they desecrate Lamia's " secret bowers " (II. 149) and " spoil her solitude " (II. 145), the secret presence of the mystery, which was, like the nymph, invisible until Lycius was inwardly impelled to display it.

Only now does Apollonius make his appearance. He has not burst into the vision and destroyed it. Only when Lycius has opened the palace to the world of the senses, has taken on a proper self, and has mastered Lamia, can Apollonius enter. He is an uninvited guest, but only when the ideal vision is humanized does the conceptual mind intrude and reduce the mysterious to the understandable; and once it is possible for Apollonius to enter, Lycius himself, although embarrassed, leads the old man " through the inner doors broad-spread " (II. 170), into the heart of the mystery. The philosopher works on the " knotty problem " until it begins " to thaw, / And solve and melt " (II. 160–62) ; for, like Coleridge, he dissipates what is " caught from the Penetralium of mystery, from being incapable of remaining Content with half knowledge." [9] Apollonius' function is to preserve Lycius " from every ill / Of life " (II. 297–98) ; his duty is to call out, " La Belle Dame sans Merci / Hath thee in thrall! " for his concern is only the mortal Lycius. As Lycius' conceptual brain, it is his duty to make all charms—all ideal visions of the mystery—disappear. And consequently by the penetration of his glance he makes fade and disappear the Cynthia-like beauty of Lamia until only the earthliness of beauty is left, that earthliness being the serpent, the ugliness, the pain.

Keats lamented that " ' In our unimaginative days ' " we have been " Habeas Corpus'd . . . out of all wonder, curiosity, and fear;—in these fire-side, delicate, gilded days,—these days of sickly safety and comfort." [10] He lamented that " The goblin is is driven from the hearth, and the rainbow is robbed of its mystery." [11] He complained that Newton " had destroyed all the poetry of the rainbow by reducing it to the prismatic colours." [12] But in " Lamia " he was facing squarely the unpleasant fact that

[9] Letter to George and Thomas Keats, December 21, 1817.
[10] " On Edmund Kean as a Shakespearian Actor."
[11] *Ibid.*
[12] *The Poetical Works . . . of John Keats,* ed. H. B. Forman (London, 1883), IV. 353.

mortal man cannot avoid creating the conditions that allow the conceptual mind to intrude and

> *Conquer all mysteries by rule and line,*
> *Empty the haunted air, and gnomed mine—*
> *Unweave a rainbow, as it erewhile made*
> *The tender-person'd Lamia melt into a shade.*

(II. 235–38)

For, although " Scanty the hour and few the steps beyond the bourn of care," there is a check on man's journeys heavenward so that " at the cable's length / Man feels the gentle anchor pull." [13]

---

[13] " Lines Written in the Highlands after a Visit to Burns's Country," 29, 39-40.

Ode to a Nightingale

I

My heart aches, and a drowsy numbness pains
　My sense, as though of hemlock I had drunk,
Or emptied some dull opiate to the drains
　One minute past, and Lethe-wards had sunk:
'Tis not through envy of thy happy lot,　　　　　　　　5
　But being too happy in thine happiness,—
　　That thou, light-winged Dryad of the trees,
　　　In some melodious plot
　Of beechen green, and shadows numberless,
　　Singest of summer in full-throated ease.　　　　10

II

O, for a draught of vintage! that hath been
　Cool'd a long age in the deep-delved earth,
Tasting of Flora and the country green,
　Dance, and Provençal song, and sunburnt mirth!
O for a beaker full of the warm South,　　　　　　15
　Full of the true, the blushful Hippocrene,
　　With beaded bubbles winking at the brim,
　　　And purple-stained mouth;
That I might drink, and leave the world unseen,
　And with thee fade away into the forest dim:　　20

III

Fade far away, dissolve, and quite forget
　What thou among the leaves hast never known,
The weariness, the fever, and the fret
　Here, where men sit and hear each other groan;
Where palsy shakes a few, sad, last gray hairs,　　25
　Where youth grows pale, and spectre-thin, and dies;
　　Where but to think is to be full of sorrow

[175]

And leaden-eyed despairs,
Where Beauty cannot keep her lustrous eyes,
Or new Love pine at them beyond to-morrow.   30

IV

Away! away! for I will fly to thee,
Not charioted by Bacchus and his pards,
But on the viewless wings of Poesy,
Though the dull brain perplexes and retards:
Already with thee! tender is the night,   35
And haply the Queen-Moon is on her throne,
Cluster'd around by all her starry Fays;
But here there is no light,
Save what from heaven is with the breezes blown
Through verdurous glooms and winding mossy ways.   40

V

I cannot see what flowers are at my feet,
Nor what soft incense hangs upon the boughs,
But, in embalmed darkness, guess each sweet
Wherewith the seasonable month endows
The grass, the thicket, and the fruit-tree wild;   45
White hawthorn, and the pastoral eglantine;
Fast fading violets cover'd up in leaves;
And mid-May's eldest child,
The coming musk-rose, full of dewy wine,
The murmurous haunt of flies on summer eves.   50

VI

Darkling I listen; and, for many a time
I have been half in love with easeful Death,
Call'd him soft names in many a mused rhyme,
To take into the air my quiet breath;
Now more than ever seems it rich to die,   55
To cease upon the midnight with no pain,
While thou art pouring forth thy soul abroad
In such an ecstasy!

Still wouldst thou sing, and I have ears in vain—
  To thy high requiem become a sod.   60

VII

Thou wast not born for death, immortal Bird!
  No hungry generations tread thee down;
The voice I hear this passing night was heard
  In ancient days by emperor and clown:
Perhaps the self-same song that found a path   65
    Through the sad heart of Ruth, when, sick for home,
      She stood in tears amid the alien corn;
        The same that oft-times hath
Charm'd magic casements, opening on the foam
  Of perilous seas, in faery lands forlorn.   70

VIII

Forlorn! the very word is like a bell
  To toll me back from thee to my sole self!
Adieu! the fancy cannot cheat so well
  As she is fam'd to do, deceiving elf.
Adieu! adieu! thy plaintive anthem fades   75
    Past the near meadows, over the still stream,
      Up the hill-side; and now 'tis buried deep
        In the next valley-glades:
Was it a vision, or a waking dream?
  Fled is that music:—Do I wake or sleep?   80

Ode to a Nightingale

O<small>F ALL</small> Keats' poems, it is probably the " Ode to a Nightingale " that has most tormented the critic. The " Ode on a Grecian
Urn " may trouble (unnecessarily, I think) because of the identification of beauty and truth, but even an uncritical reading of that
ode leaves one with the sense that the poet himself, at any rate,
has arrived at the end of his making with all passion spent.
Through the poet's engagement in the struggle the poetic storm
appears to have been hushed into a calm that gives him a new
resolution, a firmer grasp of values than he had before his ship-
wrecked journey in search of a Northwest Passage. But in any
reading of the " Ode to a Nightingale " the turmoil will not down.
Forces contend wildly within the poem, not only without resolution,
but without possibility of resolution ; and the reader comes away
from his experience with the sense that he has been in a

> *wild Abyss,*
> *The Womb of nature and perhaps her Grave,*
> *Of neither Sea, nor Shore, nor Air, nor Fire,*
> *But all these in their pregnant causes mixt*
> *Confusedly.*

It is this turbulence, I suspect, that has led Allen Tate to
believe the ode " at least tries to say everything that poetry can
say." [1] But I propose it is the " Ode on a Grecian Urn " that succeeds in saying what poetry can say, and that the other ode attempts to say all that the *poet* can. For the first is self-contained
art : it develops out of its initial situation by an inner compulsion,

---

[1] *On the Limits of Poetry* (New York, 1948), 168.

and works out its own destiny in terms of its inherent drama, its own grammar and symbols. Its dynamic force lies within itself and is released and exploited by factors that are the property of poetry alone, and of this poem in particular: rhythm, tempo, rhyme, syntax, grammatical gesture, the self-impelled movement of the images. It therefore satisfies Coleridge's definition of a legitimate poem: " one, the parts of which mutually support and explain each other; all in their proportion harmonizing with, and supporting the purpose and known influences of metrical arrangement." [2] But the second poem is synthetically fashioned: instead of operating within its own framework, it functions only because the poet intervenes and cuts across the grain of his materials to make them vibrant. The first is the poetic cosmos; the second is the poet's chaos. The first is the work of art; the second the workings of art. By these large generalizations I do not mean to imply a value judgment, but simply to put the two poems into different categories, despite their very great similarities in subject matter, procedure, and conceptual intent. What value judgments we make must take into consideration these categorical differences.

Many of our difficulties in interpreting the " Ode to a Nightingale " no doubt arise from a foresight born of long familiarity. Coming to the poem with a previous acquaintance in mind, we tend to read into each part the total intent. For example, we probably are inclined to think of the nightingale as an " immortal bird " even in the first stanza, and consequently contribute to the symbol considerably more than its activity at the moment justifies. But Keats' poetry is seldom static, and the nightingale does not have a fixed value throughout the poem: meaning lies not only in a symbol or a situation, but often more significantly in the direction being taken by any of the materials. The poetry is, in other words, dramatic and evolutionary, and we must read not only what is

[2] *Biographia Literaria,* ed. Shawcross, II. 10.

explicitly enacted but also what is implied by the abstract pattern made by the development of Keats' materials—their becomingness. The nightingale, for example, not only embodies a series of increasing symbolic values but also, by this act, traces out a sequentiality which is itself symbolic.

If, now, we search the poem for its most embracing active elements, we find that the two major actors are the poet and the nightingale, and that the poem elaborates a series of relationships of these two as a consequence of three proposals made by the poet. What I intend first, therefore, is not to observe the dramatic interaction of these elements, but to examine independently the courses taken by each of the dramatic threads of which the ode is woven, in order to discover what meaning may reside in the following abstract patterns: (1) the three proposals whereby the poet seeks to ease the pain of his " happiness "; (2) the symbolic significances of the nightingale; and (3) the capacities of the poet for intense experience.

ii

The conflict out of which the ode is born is a recurrent one in Keats' poetry and is the inevitable result of the oxymoronic ontology within which he thinks. The poet's self has been caught up in empathic ecstasy so completely that he is " too happy." The absorption into essence—the fellowship divine which constitutes " happiness "—has been greater than is destined for mortal man, and the result is heartache and painful numbness. The ideal condition towards which Keats always strives because it is his ideal, is one in which mortal and immortal, dynamism and stasis, the Dionysian and the Apollonian, beauty and truth, are one. And in the " Ode on a Grecian Urn " and " La Belle Dame Sans Merci " he had traced mortal man's momentary ascent to, and his inevitable eviction from, this condition. But if, in his aspirations towards the

conditions of heaven's bourne, man is unable to draw heaven and
earth together into a stable union—and it is part of Keats' scheme
of things that he must be unable while he is mortal—then he is torn
between the two extremes, grasping after both but at home in
neither. Even in the ode on the urn, where the material and the
ethereal did for a moment coalesce, they quickly separated out of
their volatile union.   Therefore,

> *O that our dreamings all of sleep or wake*
> *Would all their colours from the Sunset take:*
> *From something of material sublime,*
> *Rather than shadow our own Soul's daytime*
> *In the dark void of Night. For in the world*
> *We jostle. . . .*
>
> *. . . Oh never will the prize,*
> *High reason, and the lore of good and ill*
> *Be my award. Things cannot to the will*
> *Be settled, but they tease us out of thought.*
> *Or is it that Imagination brought*
> *Beyond its proper bound, yet still confined,—*
> *Lost in a sort of Purgatory blind,*
> *Cannot refer to any standard law*
> *Of either earth or heaven?—It is a flaw*
> *In happiness to see beyond our bourn—*
> *It forces us in Summer skies to mourn:*
> *It spoils the singing of the Nightingale.*[3]

If man could confine his aspirations to this physical world, to
" something of material sublime," he might find a degree of content; but it is of his very nature that, unless he limits himself to the
" level chambers " of mere revelry, he can no more renounce his
quest for the ideal than Endymion can renounce his quest for
Cynthia. Peona may convincingly describe the rewards of the
world, but Endymion must still yearn for an immortality of passion
and a love that makes " Men's being mortal, immortal." Once

[3] " To J. H. Reynolds, Esq.," 67-85.

mortal man has glimpsed into heaven's bourne, the physical loses its splendor and charm: awakening from a vision of Cynthia, Endy·mion found that

> deepest shades
> *Were deepest dungeons; heaths and sunny glades*
> *Were full of pestilent light,*

and that

> *all the pleasant hues*
> *Of heaven and earth had faded.*[4]

The fellowship with essence leaves only discontent with human life and spoils the singing of the nightingale.

It is inevitable, then, that men who are not merely brutish should strain to become " More happy than betides mortality "[5] and consequently be " too happy to be glad."[6] Man must always seek to ease the burden of the mystery; and since the mystery does not lie in the conceptual world, where an act of will can seize only the outward nature of things, it teases us " out of thought," tempting man to dodge conception until he is struggling against his mortal bonds. He must agonize to burst the bars that keep his spirit in.[7] Yet, man is of the earth—" For in the world / We jostle "—and he is bound to its nature, which is not perfectible: " The nature of the world will not admit of it—the inhabitants of the world will correspond to itself."[8] There can be no heaven on earth. Consequently, the heavenward flight of an earth-bound mortal must necessarily leave him in a gulf between the two worlds, one dead, the other powerless to be born. Striving to interknit his brain " With the glory and grace of Apollo," Keats had found that

> *To thee my soul is flown,*
> *And my body is earthward press'd.*

---

[4] *Endymion*, I. 691-94.   [6] *Ibid.*, 819.
[5] *Ibid.*, IV. 859.   [7] *Ibid.*, II. 185-86.
[8] Letter to George and Georgiana Keats, February 14–May 3, 1819.

It is an awful mission,
A terrible division;
And leaves a gulph austere
To be fill'd with worldly fear.
Aye, when the soul is fled
To high above our head,
Affrighted do we gaze
After its airy maze,
As doth a mother wild,
When her young infant child
Is in an eagle's claws—
And is not this the cause
Of madness? [9]

To look at these passages in another way, Keats is here examining the consequences of the act of ecstasy, the most intense empathic entrance into essence; for since " happiness " lies in the oxymoronic nature of heaven's bourne, it can be experienced only by the annihilation of self. Yet, while man is mortal the projection of self cannot be complete because the spirit cannot wholly leave behind the sensory substance in which it is encased; the effort to nourish life's self by its proper pith must torment the sensory clay. By attempting to gain " happiness," one is brought beyond his proper bound, and yet, being mortal, he is still confined to the earthly; and thus he is left with no standards to which to refer, or rather, with two conflicting sets of standards.

It is precisely in this maddening " Purgatory blind " that is neither earth nor heaven, and from which both seem without their pleasant hues, that the " Ode to a Nightingale " has its being. It is a poem without any standard law to which to refer, oscillating between heaven and earth and never able to reconcile them. The ode begins after the point that had been attained in the third stanza of the " Ode on a Grecian Urn." That poem, by enacting the ascent

[9] " God of the Meridian."

to a condition of happiness, could then salvage from the shattered momentary experience the meaning that the extra-human ascent has in the context of human existence; the " Ode to a Nightingale," however, by beginning with the dissolution itself, can only trace its further disintegration. It is necessary to recognize clearly this initial condition of the poet, for the significance of the entire poem is dependent upon it. Because the poem begins after the height of the empathic experience and traces the further journey homeward to habitual self, we are to look for irreconcilables, not harmonies; for patterns flying apart, not coming together; for conflicting standards.

Briefly, we are to read it by an inversion of the perspectives that give the " Ode on a Grecian Urn " its meaning. Or, better, we are to recognize the irony whereby Keats translates the experience with the nightingale into the terms of one who is being drawn back to the mortal world, and not one who, as in the other ode, is progressing towards the bourne of heaven. The thematic materials of the two odes, we shall see, are the same; but what blends organically in the " Ode on a Grecian Urn " disintegrates in this ode; what is seen in its immortal aspects in the former is seen in its mortal aspects in the latter.

This inversion is easily illustrated in the opening lines of the ode, for they establish the pattern that the poem is to follow. The pleasure thermometer that Keats outlined in *Endymion* is a series of increasing intensities that result in one's selflessly becoming assimilated into essence. As the experiences become more exquisite one is more free of his physical self and the dimensional world until at last he lives in essence. These two apparently contradictory acts—extremely vigorous sensation and the destruction of the self which experiences the sensations—are, nevertheless, a single and indivisible act; and in the " Ode on a Grecian Urn " the poet was absorbed into the life within the frieze in proportion as his own passions grew into ecstasy.

But let us now invert this movement. As we retreat from passionate selflessness, the two elements separate out of their organic union into strong emotion and a loss of self. And if then we evaluate these two, not as they carry us towards the dynamic stasis of heaven, but as they appear within the framework of merely mortal experience, the powerful emotion becomes only painfully exquisite sensation, and the selflessness only a swooning unresponsiveness. A drowsy numbness that pains the senses, paradoxical though it may seem, probably has some sound basis in psychological fact; but simply to psychologize the statement without reference to Keats' ideological system will not open the poem to us. It is necessary to see that in the dissolution of ecstasy into heartache and numbness the oxymoronic nature of Keats' ideal has begun to disintegrate into its component parts and that the poet's interpretation of his experience is being distorted by his translation of it into the concepts of the mortal world. What should be thrilling intensity is an intensity of the wrong kind—only the ache of the heart and the pain of the senses; what should be ecstatic selflessness is the wrong kind of selflessness—only drowsy numbness, a slipping Lethe-wards, something comparable to drinking hemlock or a dull opiate. And instead of blending mystically, intensity and selflessness struggle against each other irreconcilably. Ideally, intensities enthrall the self; here the ideal is inverted: numbness pains the sense. In this dichotomy and inversion are contained all the workings of the poem, for the poet's effort to resolve his inner conflict by seeking ease will further split the elements of the poem into tense contrarieties.

In the first stanza there are two of these conflicts: the one we have been examining that fractures the poet's " happiness " into pain and numbness; and the antithesis of the two empathies, the poet's and the nightingale's, an antithesis of two " happinesses " that determines the structure of the stanza. The poet's heart aches, we

are told, not because he envies the happiness of the nightingale—
envy being the reverse of empathy; but because he has himself
entered too deeply into the empathic happiness of the nightingale—
is "too happy in thine happiness." For such selfless participation
in essence is not designed for mortal man. He has ascended the
pleasure thermometer as high as merely human powers permit, but
there is nothing to fix his intensity there, nothing to remove its
temporality, no heaven's bourne into which to empty it. The consequence is a drowsy ache like that of Porphyro, who, about to rise
"Beyond a mortal man impassion'd far," complains to the sleeping
Madeline, the "completed form" with whom he is to blend and
so become mortally immortal:

> *Open thine eyes, for meek St. Agnes' sake,*
> *Or I shall drowse beside thee, so my soul doth ache.*

For Porphyro, too, what should be an impassioned selflessness
threatens to become its human correlative, a drowsiness and an
ache. The nightingale, on the other hand, is as self-annihilated as
the poet, for it has entered into the essence of nature, the sense of
its empathic indwelling being reinforced by its being a "Dryad,"
a nymph whose life is that of the tree she inhabits. Yet this
empathy allows it to sing, not with mortal pain, but in "full-
throated ease." The setting of the ode is mid-May, as stanza five
will make clear, and yet the song the bird sings is one of summer,
that period in the temporal world when the inner essence of nature
comes to fruition and becomes manifest. The summer of which the
bird sings is the full and timeless essence of nature, while spring
is only that essence operating in the temporal context of becoming.
Nevertheless, although it is spring, the bird is so absorbed into
nature's inwardness that it knows its perfection, which, in the
temporal world, is the point towards which and from which nature
is always moving, but which, in the immortal, is fixed and changeless. The nightingale, then, is like Pan, to whom

Ode to a Nightingale

Broad leaved fig trees even now foredoom
Their ripen'd fruitage. . . .
The chuckling linnet its five young unborn,
To sing for thee. . .
. . . pent up butterflies
Their freckled wings; yea, the fresh budding year
All its completions.[10]

For, being a firmament reflected in a sea, Pan is one with the heart of nature, and nature belongs to him, not in its becoming, its spring, but in its full and changelessly vital being, its " completions "—its summer. In another sense, too, this empathic union with nature is complete: the bird is deep *in* nature—among the shadows of the plot of trees; and nature itself is saturated with the sound of the bird—the plot of beechen green has taken on the quality of the bird to become " melodious." And yet, the nightingale is able to attain this perfect " happiness " in ease, whereas such spiritual projection by the poet—his happiness *in* the nightingale's—produces pain.

Only in the central two lines of the first stanza (5-6) are the three elements of the ode—the poet, the nightingale, and nature—integrated, although not harmoniously. The bird has entered into the essence of nature, and the poet into the essence of the bird. The empathic relationships embodied in these two lines are precisely those attained in the third stanza of the " Ode on a Grecian Urn "; for there the three symbols had attained " happiness " in arriving at a condition in which love is forever warm and still to be enjoyed, and the poet had revealed his absorption into their happiness by the ecstasy of his exclamations: " More happy, happy love! " But the first stanza of the ode to a nightingale sharply juxtaposes the two empathies, pivoting them on these two central lines: the weighty and sluggish movement of the opening four lines

[10] *Endymion*, I. 251-60.

conveys the dull ache of the poet's unnatural strain; the exhausting flow of the last four lines, the natural ease with which the bird participates in essence.

We now have the seminal elements of the poem. The opposition of pain and numbness in the poet must seek out a resolution. The juxtaposition of the two empathies excites the instability of the poet's condition, for the perfection of the nightingale's happiness underscores the uneasiness of the poet's, which must now fall apart into the two incompatible elements of which it is compacted: spirit and matter, heaven and earth, the immortal and the mortal. The poem will now develop by two crisscrossing movements: the enervation of the poet's passion as he seeks ease from pain; and the increasing intensity of the bird's symbolic values. As the poet moves downward from the bird towards mortality in an effort to capture the bird's ease, he will see the bird as symbolizing proportionately higher levels of meaning. The first stanza therefore appropriately ends on the word "ease," which, like the word "ecstasy" (the antonym of "ease") at the end of the first stanza of the "Ode on a Grecian Urn," contains the motive of what is to follow. Ease appears to belong to the bird's empathy; and the poet, being misguided, will seek to capture it to resolve the pain-numbness conflict of his own empathy.

The condition created in the first stanza also contains in itself the proposals whereby the poet will vainly strive to free his happiness from pain. In the drinking of the hemlock, the deep draught of the opiate, the slipping Lethe-wards, the earthiness and warmth of the bird's singing of summer, and the full-throated ease—in all these is foreshadowed the desire for forgetfulness by drinking the warm and mature earthiness of wine. Transformed by the theme of wine, the beechen green will become the country green; the melodious plot, Provençal song; and the shadows numberless, the deep-delved earth. Second, that the light-winged Dryad is singing a song of essence suggests the proposal to fly to heaven's bourne on the " viewless wings of Poesy." And finally, the drowsy numbness, the poisonous hemlock, the Lethe-ward movement, and the sense of shadowy darkness anticipate the proposal of death. The elements of the entire drama are, therefore, inherent in the opening stanza: it creates an unstable situation—the conflict within the poet—which must seek out a resolution; it dramatically contrasts this instability with the ideal happiness of the nightingale to give it depth and meaning; it thereby sets in motion two countercurrents; and it contains implicitly the three stages of the course these countercurrents will take. The poem will now proceed, not with dramatic inevitability, but by a series of jolting transformations whereby the three elements of the ode—the poet, the nightingale, and nature— will be shaken into a succession of different relationships.

iii

To turn now to the first of the dramatic strands: the proposals whereby the poet will seek to free his " happiness " of mortal pain and to experience what appears to him to be the ease of the nightingale—wine, poesy, and death. In Keats' system of symbolic perceptions, wine had come to represent to him sensuous pleasure for its own sake. It seemed to promise a sensuous intensity, it is true, but one that, instead of leading to a self-annihilation through the projection of self into essence, leads only to a forgetfulness of self. It is, then, a false sort of self-destruction, for it ends only in that self-destruction and not in an interknitting with life's proper pith. " Happy " boughs symbolize sensory fellowship with essence, for in them lies " happiness," the power of beckoning man to essence; but wine symbolizes this sensuous act as merely mortal man would interpret it, for to him the pleasure seems to be its own end. When, for example, the Indian Maiden followed Bacchus and his crew she experienced the entire range of earthly pleasures and yet was " Sick hearted, weary ":

> *I've been a ranger*
> *In search of pleasure throughout every clime:*
> *Alas! 'tis not for me!* [11]

For there is a difference between pleasure and " happiness," just as it is possible to be " too happy to be glad." Keats may have painted a glamorous and appealing picture of dance and Provençal song, but this mere gaiety was worthless in his scheme of values:

> *The Muse should never make the spirit gay;*
> *Away, bright dulness, laughing fools away.* [12]

In " The Eve of St. Agnes " the baron and his guests are all those who are so deep in the revelries of the world that the pleasures of the senses are ends in themselves, and therefore these creatures are confined to the " level chambers " of life. They are " Drown'd all in Rhenish and the sleepy mead "; they are the " bloated wassail-lers " who, because of their concern with mere sensuous delight, " will never heed " the passage of Porphyro and Madeline into the mystery of the elfin-storm. The satyrs and sileni, followers of Bacchus, seeing only the physical beauty of Hermes' nymph, made her immortality grow pale by the " love-glances of their unlovely eyes "—their delight in the sensuous without even a recognition of the essence that lies in the sensuous. Finally, the Corinthian world which appears at the wedding of Lamia and Lycius—the " herd " with " common eyes "—luxuriates in the riches of the senses : " the cold full sponge to pleasure press'd," the fragrant oils. And the enthrallment by the wine, instead of leading to a sensuous fellow-ship with essence, makes the world-guests in the magic palace

[11] *Ibid.*, IV. 269, 274-76.
[12] " The Eve of St. Agnes," stanza 5, variant.

oblivious not only to human pain but also to the mystery in whose presence they stand : the mystery was,

> *Now, when the wine has done its rosy deed,*
> *And every soul from human trammels freed,*
> *No more so strange; for merry wine, sweet wine,*
> *Will make Elysian shades not too fair, too divine.*
>
> (II. 209–12)

In the ode, then, wine is a symbol of the misguided effort to engage in the sensory essence of nature without pain; a beguiling hope of penetrating to the inwardness of the sensory in such a way as to be at ease in empathy; a worldly illusion that fellowship with sensuous essence is only a distracting pleasure. At first glance the proposal seems especially appropriate to the poetic situation that has been created. The ease of the nightingale appears to arise out of the perfect interpenetration of its essence with that of nature. The bird sings of the soul of nature, " of summer "; and nature is inhabited by the soul of the bird—the bird is within the shadows, and the plot is " melodious " with the bird's spirit, its song. So, too, the wine has been cooled *in* the depths of earth, and *in* it is the taste of the country green. Superficially, it appears that it is in the essence of earthiness, and that the essence of earthiness is in it. Moreover, like the ease of the bird, only pleasures are contained in the wine: a " sunburnt mirth " and the " warm South " which holds out the false promise of being the same completeness of nature into which the bird, in singing of summer, has insight. The parallelism of the nightingale and the wine is, of course, a false parallelism and suggests itself to the poet only because he is facing earthward. Wine has the illusory appearance of being a means of gaining the bird's easeful empathy only because he is looking on outward forms and is negligent of spiritual values.

There is no need to linger over the significance and appropriateness of the second proposal. " I am certain of nothing," Keats

wrote, " but of the holiness of the Heart's affections and the truth
of Imagination—What the imagination seizes as Beauty must be
truth." [13] The imagination functions by projecting the self into the
beauty, the vital essence of its objective, and thereby sees that
essence in terms of its eternal being in heaven's bourne. The
imagination, therefore, allows a pre-enactment, an earthly rehearsal,
of the " happiness " to come. Ideally, then, poesy should provide a
true happiness, a perfect fellowship with essence without a mortal
heartache. The imagination does not merely look on outer forms
but penetrates to the central life of what it deals with, just as the
nightingale is able to sing of summer, the central life of nature.
The poet, therefore, is

> *the man who with a bird,*
> *Wren or Eagle, finds his way to*
> *All its instincts; he hath heard*
> *The Lion's roaring, and can tell*
> *What his horny throat expresseth,*
> *And to him the Tiger's yell*
> *Comes articulate and presseth*
> *On his ear like mother-tongue.*[14]

To the sight of the poet

> *The husk of natural objects opens quite*
> *To the core: and every secret essence there*
> *Reveals the elements of good and fair;*
> *Making him see, where Learning hath no light.*[15]

But again the metaphysical premises of the ode go awry. Poesy,
which should open up the essence of nature and make it one with
the poet's self, fails to function as it ideally should; and once again
what should lead to the bourne of heaven is transformed into the

[13] Letter to Bailey, November 22, 1817.
[14] " Where's the Poet? "
[15] " The Poet " ("At morn, at noon, at Eve, and Middle Night ").

merely mundane: " I cannot see what flowers are at my feet." The husk of natural objects refuses to open to the core.

It is fairly clear why wine and the poetic imagination should have appeared appropriate means of resolving the painful numbness into an easy empathy, but it may not be equally clear why these two proposals should finally suggest death. These first two proposals, it will be noticed, are approximately the same as the initial stages of a procedural pattern that had become a fixed part of Keats' ways of thinking. The aspiration towards a selfless, spaceless immortality of passion which Keats saw as the promised post-mortal life, and which he agonized to capture in this present existence, had fashioned for itself a clearly marked route which he once called the pleasure thermometer. The first two stages on that route—entrance into the essence of nature and art, or the exertion of the intensities of the senses and of the imagination—are here symbolized by wine (falsely) and by poetry (ineffectually). And if Keats is once again molding a poem into the pattern of his spiritual epistemology, as we have seen him do repeatedly, he should then seek mystical union with essence through love. Indeed, there is reason to believe that something of the original pattern of the pleasure thermometer still lingers in Keats' mind. For the poet addresses death in terms of love: he has been half in love with death; and in tenderly worded poetry, addressing him by " soft names," he has, like a lover, begged him to take up the poet's spirit.

But it is possible to see even more clearly why Keats now conceives of death instead of love as the last and highest stage of the pleasure thermometer. In the sonnet " Why did I laugh to-night? " he could not gain from heaven or hell or his own heart an explanation of the laugh. What meaning, he is asking, does this moment of joy have in the total design of his life, its pleasures and sufferings? To what end are being shaped the apparently fortuitous gladnesses and pains to which we are subjected in this life? The answer lies in the Mystery alone: " O Darkness! Darkness! ever must I moan, / To question Heaven and Hell and Heart in vain." Now, Keats was no " Godwin perfectibility Man." The full measure of happiness is not to be found in this world, nor could it ever be; and mortal man is therefore made to suffer:

> suppose a rose to have sensation, it blooms on a beautiful morning it enjoys itself—but there comes a cold wind, a hot sun—it cannot escape it, it cannot destroy its annoyances— they are as native to the world as itself: no more can man be happy in spite, the worldly elements will prey upon his nature.[16]

Even granted such earthly happiness, man " is mortal and there is still a heaven with its Stars above his head." Were there earthly perfectibility, " the whole troubles of life which are now frittered away in a series of years, would the[n] be accumulated for the last days of a being who instead of hailing its approach, would leave this world as Eve left Paradise." The pain that lies in mortal pleasures, the melancholy that has her shrine in the temple of delight, the burning forehead and the parching tongue that attend upon human passions—these must have a meaning and a function in the total scheme of one's being.

On the other hand, Keats could not accept what he understood to be the Christian scheme: " The common cognomen of this world among the misguided and superstitious is ' a vale of tears ' from which we are to be redeemed by a certain arbitrary interposition of God and taken to Heaven—What a little circumscribed straightened notion ! " Pain is not to be overcome in this life, nor is pain a penalty for sin, from which we are to be redeemed by happiness in a future state. There must be, Keats felt, a closer interconnection of experience than this. The burning forehead must come with the passion, and it must therefore have a part to play in the progress

[16] Letter to George and Georgiana Keats, February 14–May 3, 1819.

[194]

towards the bourne of heaven; for the future is not the inverse of
the present, but the present divested of its mutability. Existence is
a continuum, part of which endures pain and mutability; but since
it is a continuum, all that occurs in this life is functionally progressive towards the next. Therefore (to return to the sonnet), although the poet knows the utmost blisses of his worldly existence,
yet would he " on this very midnight cease " because

> *Verse, Fame, and Beauty are intense indeed,*
> *But Death intenser—Death is Life's high meed.*

We can now see the position of death in the pleasure thermometer. Nature, art, and love are increasing intensities, and in
proportion as they enthrall the spirit they interknit it with essence.
But the " Richer entanglements, enthralments far / More self-
destroying," Keats has said, lead by degrees " To the chief intensity," which is beyond even love. Death, then, is not an event
which divides two existences, but the meeting point at which the
ladder of intensities enters heaven's bourne. It is the final intensity
at the very verge of immortal life that shatters the " fragile bar /
That keeps us from our homes ethereal " and places us in Intensity
itself, where at last life's self is perpetually nourished by its own
essence. Because death is the climax of these " *richer* entanglements "—indeed is the one whereby the self is totally enthralled—
" now more than ever seems it *rich* to die." In his sonnet " Bright
star ! " we have seen, Keats longed for the steadfastness of the
star, but not its lone splendor; he wished for its unchangeableness,
but only if it would be fused with an intensity of passion:

> *yet still steadfast, still unchangeable,*
> *Pillow'd upon my fair love's ripening breast,*
> *To feel for ever its soft fall and swell,*
> *Awake for ever in a sweet unrest,*
> *Still, still to hear her tender-taken breath,*
> *And so live ever. . . .*

This, of course, is the oxymoronic condition of heaven's bourne experienced on earth—the becomingness of "ripening," the mutability of the passionate fall and swell, caught up in a changeless foreverness. Keats then continues,

And so live ever—or else swoon to death.

His meaning is not that if he cannot capture on earth an immortality of passion he may as well not exist at all, but that death, the last earthly intensity, is an alternative and final source of an immortality of passion. That this is his intent is clear in an earlier version of the last line:

Half-passionless, and so swoon on to death.

It is, therefore, towards death that all our earthly existence is leading. The intensities of pain and pleasure reach their final earthly degree in death; thus death is "Life's high meed," for it raises us to the ultimate Intensity, which is without degree, and it gives a meaning to our mortal experiences, even a random laugh.

In constructing in the ode another version of the pleasure thermometer, Keats has substituted for love the last earthly degree beyond love; and the progress from wine to poesy to death— the absorption of the sensuous, the imaginative, and finally the total spiritual self—should, unless the poet is beguiled, lead to one's capture in heaven's bourne and therefore to a "happiness" with ease. But once again the poet has mistaken Duessa for Fidessa: in desiring release from pain he has proposed a false view of death. The death that shatters the bar to admit the self into immortality is an intensity, an exquisite experience; but the poet here, although it seems *rich* to die, has limited his vision to the physical and sensory world, and from that perspective he asks only for an easeful death, a cessation with no pain. This is the worldly inverse of death in its immortal aspect, and because the poet is facing earthward instead of heavenward, such a view of death reveals, not an absorption of self into the immortal spirit of life, but only a physical decay. In a merely worldly framework, death is release from pain and eventuates in one's becoming a sod, a part of inanimate nature. The design that underlies the three proposals is drawn from the pleasure thermometer, but the scale of intensities is grotesquely distorted by being seen through the eyes of, let us say, the baron and his fellow revelers, or the guests in Lamia's palace. The axis on which Keats' universe rotates has been bent awry, and his entire scheme of things is being shaken apart.

iv

Each of these three proposals for empathic union brings about a reorientation of relationships among the poet, the nightingale, and the world of physical reality; and with each of these transformations the nightingale appears to take on additional degrees of symbolic value. The nightingale with whom the poem begins is, we have seen, an embodiment of the perfect empathy which the poet seeks. But the description reveals only that the bird has succeeded where the poet fails: each attains the same degree of empathic happiness, except that it is commensurate with the bird's capacity and so much beyond the poet's that it leads to an unpleasant separation of its components, a painful swooning of the senses. It is not in any way implied that the bird belongs to an order of things different from that of the poet, but only that the two are experiencing the same kind of " happiness " with contrary results.

Now in each successive transformation the nightingale seems to the poet to rise in the scale of values. When the poet proposes to release himself from the pain of his ecstasy by becoming one with the sensuous essence of physical nature, he finds (in stanza three) that the bird is now outside the context of physical nature:

it has never known the weariness, the fever, and the fret which are inextricable from the world of extensions. But this is only a negative distinction; we know only that the nightingale now seems to belong to an order of things which is not the poet's.

(Before we follow this movement further, it will be necessary to clear away, parenthetically, one textual crux. The line "Already with thee! tender is the night" (35) has generally been read as meaning that the poet finally succeeds in becoming united with the nightingale, and that he then finds the night to be tender. But such a reading can lead only to inconsistencies, if not to nonsense. The problem of the poet is not to get *to* the nightingale; he was, indeed, already absorbed into the bird's soul when the poem opened. His problem is how to convert that painful happiness into a happiness with ease, and something has happened meanwhile that has been dissolving the empathic union. The successive efforts of the poet to relieve the pain separate him farther from the symbol, and the whole dramatic direction of the poem is towards a further divorce, not towards a reunion. Moreover, there would be no meaning in the poet's complaint that " here there is no light " and that he cannot see the flowers at his feet, for if he is with the bird he should be able to see into essence as vividly as the bird can sing of summer, and he should be as much in the presence of the Queen-Moon as he supposes the bird is.

(I am convinced, therefore, that Mr. Clyde S. Kilby [17] is right in suggesting that the exclamation mark after " thee " is not terminal—although I would not accept his proposal that it should be removed in our reading of the line. The exclamation mark must be introduced only to underscore the word " thee " and thereby to emphasize the contrast between " with thee " and " here " (38), which, like the " Here " of line 24, designates the

[17] *Explicator*, V (1947), no. 27.

physical world. Indeed, in one manuscript version (E), the line does read: "Already with thee tender is the night"; and the exclamation mark seems to have been introduced to transfer the emphasis from " with," where the meter would normally place it, to " thee." The night is tender with the nightingale, but it leaves the poet in blind darkness. None of the proposals, then, not even poesy, succeeds in returning the poet to empathic union with the nightingale.)

To continue with the symbolic significance of the nightingale. With the second proposal, the bird, which had been distinguished from the mutable world, is now discovered to be in the presence of ideality. Not only is the nightingale distinct from the mutable world by never having been related to its inherent principle, decay; the night, the darkness in which the mystery resides, is tender with the nightingale, and to the bird the ideal Queen-Moon is on her throne, pouring out the light of complete illumination. The moon, as Endymion discovered, is "that completed form of all completeness," the perfection of beauty-truth in its ultimate being; and when he is bathed in its light, his

> *dazzled soul*
> *Commingling with her argent spheres did roll*
> *Through clear and cloudy.*[18]

In the presence of the moon, " On some bright essence could I lean, and lull / Myself to immortality." [19] In stanza four the nightingale, then, has apparently risen to a higher level of symbolic meaning, for it is not merely distinguished from the mutable, but is perhaps (" haply ") partaking of ultimate truth, the " completeness " towards which all becoming tends and which draws one to an immortality. Moreover, the nightingale experiences the

[18] *Endymion*, I. 594-96.   [19] *Ibid.*, III. 172-73.

ideal with a perfection that earthly man cannot, for to it the Queen-Moon is not " sans merci."

However, only in the last transformation does the full symbolic meaning of the nightingale come about. It appears now to be experiencing the intensity of ecstasy, not merely a happiness with ease; it is not merely penetrating into the essence of nature—singing " of summer "—but pouring forth its spiritual essence, engaging in that total projection of spiritual self which Keats understood to be the condition of man only in heaven's bourne. Moreover, the bird is also singing a " high requiem," a song for the departed spirit. It is, then, in ecstatic union with spirit, for it is giving up its soul—its song—as mortal man will do only upon his death, and this soul-song is about the soul. The bird that originally appeared to be in fellowship with the essence of nature is now one with spiritual essence, or Essence itself. A requiem, however, is a mass that invites repose for the soul, and therefore suggests something antithetical to the vibrant restlessness of the bird's ecstasy. But the bird, indeed, is in ecstasy and yet is singing a requiem, fusing these two qualities, for the oxymoronic condition of heaven of which it sings is a vibrant repose—the rise and fall of passion fused with the star's steadfastness, an immortality of passion, beauty which is identical with truth. Having outlined the pleasure thermometer in *Endymion,* Keats described love, the highest mortal means of fellowship with essence, as an " ardent listlessness." [20] Briefly, the nightingale has appeared to be a mortal creature, has risen out of mortality, has come into the presence of beauty-truth, and has at last become a vision of beauty-truth itself—and hence is an " immortal Bird." The movement is comparable to that of the first three stanzas of the " Ode on a Grecian Urn," where the figures in the frieze rose from merely human

[20] *Ibid.,* I. 825.

passions to the conditions of heaven and at last experienced a love that is forever warm and still to be enjoyed—a condition that corresponds to the ecstasy-requiem of the nightingale.

v

The two movements we have been tracing—the false pleasure thermometer of proposals, and the ascending values of the nightingale—do not, however, give to the poem its dramatic impetus. Considered dramatically, both are inert, at no point compelling a development. Although the three proposals are implicit in the first stanza, it is not inherently inevitable that wine lead to poesy and death, and the proposals do not causally give rise to the nightingale's symbolic significances. At best, Keats can only arrange the proposals in a hierarchic order and parallel the hierarchy with ascending symbolic meanings. What gives to the poem its dramatic tension—although not a dramatic inevitability, an inner compulsion—is that the poet himself cuts across these two ascending patterns. Only in the poet himself are the nightingale and the proposals related to each other, and he imparts to them a series of dramatic tensions by following, not a corresponding ascending path, as in the " Ode on a Grecian Urn," but one of decreasing capacity for sensuous intensity. The consequence is that at no point can the three strands be in harmonious relationship, and the poem unfolds, not organically, but by an episodic series of three transformations, each transformation supplying a new layer of ironic meanings. The melody of the " Ode on a Grecian Urn " is harmonic; that of the " Ode to a Nightingale," contrapuntal.

At the opening of the poem, we have seen, the poet is at the height of his empathic power, for his enthrallment by essence is more intense than his senses can bear. His ecstatic absorption cannot possibly rise higher and is already disintegrating into an intensity which is pain and a selflessness which is numbness. The

effort to release himself from that pain by seeking the apparent
ease of the nightingale must inevitably bring about a weakening
of intensity, for it is Keats' basic assumption everywhere that
" happiness," no matter how briefly it is experienced, is exquisite
and ecstatic, not easeful. In making his first proposal in stanza
two, therefore, the poet expresses himself by an optative exclamation: " O, for a draught of vintage! " The passion is still great,
and the excited, overflowing energy of the entire stanza helps
support the intensity; but it is somewhat weaker than that of the
first stanza and is moving towards a release from the ecstatic pain.
The frozen intensity of stanza one seems to have become a fluid
violence.

In the fourth stanza, where he offers his second proposal, the
poet feels now only the passionate power of the promissory, or
the resolute: " for I will fly to thee " (31) ; and the movement from
the optative to the promissory conveys a progressive enervation, a
decreasing capacity for penetration into essence. The entire movement now comes to a close with the merely declarative form of
stanza six, which proposes the final intensity: " Now more than
ever seems it rich to die " (55). With this ebbing of passionate
power there is also introduced a note of weak uncertainty and
confusion. The poet is at first emotionally absorbed in his wish
for wine and then is determined to fly on the wings of poesy; but
already his self-confidence and assurance have begun to evaporate
amidst a series of qualifications: he believes that perhaps—
" haply "—the Queen-Moon is on her throne, he gropes about in
bewildering darkness in stanza five, he is only *half* in love with
death, it merely *seems* rich to die, and he can only speculate that
perhaps the same song was heard by Ruth.

Since only the intense passion of ecstasy allows penetration
into essence, the quest for ease that brings about these decreasing
levels of emotional power necessarily filters the poet's essence out

of the nightingale's, exactly as the poet of the " Ode on a Grecian Urn " withdrew from his absorption in the happiness of the figures in the frieze. The restless need for ease is destroying the very empathy which the poet is trying to make easeful, for it is not destined that the mortal clay be in comfort in the bourne of heaven. Consequently, although the poet in the first stanza is *in* the nightingale's happiness, he is separated out of the symbol in the second. The poet and the nightingale now occupy the same plane, but they are distinct from each other, not empathically united, and the poet hopes to fade away *with* the bird. By stanza four they are on different levels: the bird is in the presence of the moon, but " here there is no light " ; and therefore the poet now can only plan to fly *to* the nightingale. We can now see all the more clearly the inconsistency of assuming that in stanza four the poet succeeds in returning to the company of the bird, for that had already been his position in stanzas two and three, and the assumption would disrupt the progressiveness of the poet's withdrawal and destroy the meaning of the pattern.

At length, in stanza six, the poet and the nightingale have moved to opposite poles—heaven and earth—the bird addressing a spiritual song to spirit, and the poet having become a sod. The dissolution of the empathic projection is finally completed in the last stanza, where, like the poet of the ode on the Grecian urn and like the knight-at-arms, the poet is once again fully within his own individual identity: he is tolled " back *from* thee *to* my sole self." The experience of the poem is over, and it remains only for the " unpoeted " mortal to speculate on it. This drama of the poet's withdrawal and retreat, like the empathic movement in the " Ode on a Grecian Urn," has been enacted by both observable dramatic gesture and the implication of dramatic gesture through modal forms.

[203]

vi

We have dealt thus far with the increasing significances of the nightingale as though this movement were self-contained and as though the bird truly does take on greater values in its own right. But actually the nightingale is static throughout the first seven stanzas: hidden in the shadows of the trees, it continues to sing a thrilling song. It is only the descending series of intensities within the poet that gives to the nightingale its progressive meanings, for as the poet moves downward from his sensuous elevation the nightingale *seems* proportionately higher. For example, when he is merely *with* the bird spiritually in stanzas two and three, it seems unrelated to the mutable world, since the poet himself is at this moment outside the mutable world because of his still-lingering absorption into essence. But when the poet slips down to the dark world of things, the same nightingale appears to him to have risen to the presence of the Queen-Moon; and only when the poet contemplates becoming a sod does the nightingale therefore appear to be immortal. The downward movement of the poet " etherealizes " the nightingale, just as his increasing ecstasy " etherealized " the figures in the frieze of the urn.

The motivation for both of the inert sequences in the " Ode to a Nightingale " arises, then, from the poet himself: as he is drawn farther from his empathic union with the symbol, he calls upon increasingly more potent means of return, and the bird, although remaining static, appears more glorious as the poet's frame of reference is more mundane. The result is that the three strands run entirely different dramatic courses and can never come together into any resolution. At every point the nightingale outdistances the proposals: when the poet plans to ease his empathic pain with the sensuous intoxication of earthiness, the nightingale appears to belong to an order of things wholly distinct from the world of mutability; when he plans to perceive into the inwardness of nature, the nightingale is already in the presence of the light that comes from the ideal completed form of all completeness; and when he seeks release through what should be the greatest intensity, death, the nightingale is found to belong to the immortal order of things.

At the same time that the nightingale is outdistancing the false proposals, the poet himself is moving in the opposite direction, dropping counter to the intensities of his proposals and becoming progressively more remote from the symbol with which he seeks an untroubled spiritual union. By the first of his proposals for escaping mutability he hopes to participate in the vital pleasure and essential beauty of nature; by the second, to perceive into the essence of nature, but he fails; and by the third, to escape the mutable wholly, only to find that he is the insensate physical stuff of nature. In other words, with each advance up the false scale of intensities, the poet finds ironically that he is proportionately more insensate and that his attempt to free himself from the pains of the physical is binding him more inextricably to the physical. His progress is from a participation in the life of nature (to drink the earthiness of the earth-stored wine), to an unsuccessful attempt to perceive its vitality (to see into the essence of what lies at his feet), to a discovery that by his wish for death he is to become the unvital material of nature (to become the very sod that lies beneath his feet). From the perspective of the mortal world—which is the poet's perspective throughout the poem—easeful self-annihilation is to be experienced only in becoming incapable of sensation: a sod.

Yet, all the while that he is sinking earthward, his proposals are false hopes in the other direction. And while his soul is fleeing heavenward although his " body is earthward pressed," the ironic knowledge is growing that it is the nightingale, not the poet, who is progressing to heaven's bourne. Because the poet's point of view is only mortal, the progress of the figures on the urn's frieze towards heaven, when translated into mortal terms, is only a movement from town to altar; the apotheosis of the nightingale, when placed in the context of mutability, turns out to be the poet's becoming a sod.

Here, indeed, is a Purgatory blind with no standard laws of either earth or heaven, a terrible division of currents running at cross purposes. The consequence is that within the first six stanzas the poem has completely inverted itself: the ease of the nightingale's happiness, which the poet wishes for himself, rises until it becomes a pleasure-pain selflessness, an ecstasy-requiem. And the poet's numb pain has fallen away with the contemplation of " easeful Death " and of the loss of his now " quiet breath " to become " no pain "—indeed, no sensation at all, for now he has ears in vain and has become a sod. In the broadest sense, the bird's ease has become the poet's, the poet's pain has become the bird's—but with a very real difference. The poet's striving for heaven's bourne can become painless only if, in terms of mortal man, he becomes a senseless sod, for in these terms to be selfless means to be without existence. But the bird's apparently easy empathy, when seen from the perspective of this world, turns out really to be intensity itself, an ardent listlessness, beauty-truth.

If now we reconsider the three strands we have been examining we shall notice that they are, in their general outlines, precisely the same three with which Keats wove the " Ode on a Grecian Urn " and " La Belle Dame Sans Merci." We have already observed that the three proposals are false correspondences to the pleasure thermometer of intensities. The weakening of the poet's passion and his increasing separation from the happiness of the nightingale are the inverse of empathic absorption; and, by a series of transformations, the nightingale rises to an oxymoronic heaven. These are not arbitrary themes, but the three cardinal principles of

Keats' mind: his aspiration is to ascend to a condition of beauty-truth which is to be found in heaven's bourne; the pleasure thermometer is the means; and self-annihilation is the condition.

However, in both the " Ode on a Grecian Urn " and " La Belle Dame Sans Merci " these strands were not only interdependent but even inextricable from each other. In the ballad, the knight-at-arms ascended the pleasure thermometer concurrently with his increasing selflessness and thereby arrived at the elfin grot; and in the ode on the urn the emergence of the pleasure thermometer is identical with the immergence of the poet's consciousness. In the present poem the three elements are flying apart, and not only run counter to each other but are so distributed that each belongs to a different referent. The three proposals turn out to be a distorted, mundane interpretation of the pleasure thermometer; the poet's empathy, instead of increasing proportionately with the proposals, becomes less until he is wholly self-contained. And out of the crisscrossing of these two themes, it is the nightingale, not the poet, who has attained the condition of heaven. The thematic elements of the three poems are the same; but the " Ode to a Nightingale " is the obverse of the other two, a chaos to their cosmos.

vii

Having examined the three strands separately, we are now in a position to see how they are brought together in the poem, and thus to enter the poetic chaos of stanzas two through six, where the elements of a cosmos struggle " in their pregnant causes mixt Confusedly." We are not to expect that the poetic factors will reinforce each other with a nice organicism, as they do in the " Ode on a Grecian Urn." Because the poem takes place in a lawless purgatory, the elements of these stanzas will stand in ironic and illogical contradiction to each other, convulsively tossing us back and forth from nightingale to poet, from heaven to earth. They will thwart every effort at reconciliation and leave us no center of reference. Images and statements will alter in value metamorphically before our eyes and turn out to be their own converses as their referents are interchanged. And therefore the best that an explication of these stanzas can do is to set in action the bewildering oscillations.

The chaotic turmoil begins slowly, for the unit made up of stanzas two and three and motivated by the suggestion of wine has the outward appearance of a controlled structure. The first stanza of the poem had nicely juxtaposed two equal units (1-4, 7-10) to contrast the conditions of the two happinesses, one sluggishly painful, the other flowing and unruffled; and the two moods had been interlinked by the two central lines (5-6), which relate the nightingale to the essence of nature, and the poet to this essence through the essence of the nightingale, the central symbol.

This same outward form, precise, balanced, and controlled, determines the structure of stanzas two and three. Stanza two, (11–18) attempts to capture a mood resembling that of the second half of stanza one, and in tempo has nearly the same breathless, unimpeded emotional sweep. Stanza three (23–30), by means of the monotonous series (weariness, fever, fret; few, sad, last gray; pale, spectre-thin, dies; etc.) and by the dull parallelisms (where men, where palsy, where youth, where but to think, where beauty) catches something similar to the sluggish, weighty movement of the opening lines of stanza one. It is needless to underscore the other obvious contrasts between stanzas two and three: the dance opposed to the palsy and weariness; the coolness and the warm South opposed to the fever; the green floral countryside, the blushful wine, and the purple-stained mouth opposed to the leaden eyes, the pallor, and gray hairs; mirth opposed to sorrow; Provençal song opposed to groaning. These two conflicting stanzas are brought together centrally by the last two lines of stanza two and the first two lines of stanza three, which, like the central lines of stanza one, interrelate the world, the poet, and the nightingale. By this grouping, stanzas two and three, taken together, repeat the structural pattern of stanza one but invert its order; and the general, superficial impression is that the poetic world is still harmonious and intelligibly ordered.

But the forces of dissolution inherent in the poet's being " too happy " are at work even within the apparent orderliness. Not only is the proposal of the second stanza vain, since it ends in self-forgetfulness instead of self-involvement; insofar as it implies an enthrallment of the senses, it is the least intense degree of the pleasure thermometer. And yet, it is conveyed in a rhapsodic mode and with a torrential tempo; and the description is a miracle of sensuous abundance. The result is that the stanza is an organic poetic unity perfect in itself but inconsistent with the total poem. Moreover, there is a violent inconsistency in the poet's struggle in the two stanzas that make up this unit. In his present position he is with the nightingale, above the level of the mutable world, and " yet still confined " because his pain results from his being drawn earthward by his own mortal nature. From this elevated position he looks down upon the world from two inconsistent perspectives—those of heaven and earth.

Illogically, he hopes to saturate himself with the joyous and intoxicating vitality of the earth in order to free himself from the earth. He turns his back on the truth that in the world melancholy has her shrine in the temple of delight; and he hopes to split these two factors—to " unperplex bliss from its neighbour pain "—so that by being absorbed in intoxicating delight he may overcome the melancholy and decay. The fact that the wine has been deep in the earth and contains the essence of earth is a beguiling parallel to the bird, who is intimate with nature's essence and whose essence is permeating physical nature; and the illusion leads the poet to the illogical hope of similarly engaging in all the brightness of nature in order, paradoxically, to fade with the nightingale into the forest dim. Equally illogically, he hopes that by fading and dissolving he will escape the very world in which all things fade and dissolve—the world in which all men grow gray and die. And in the hope of plunging downward into the rich materials of the senses in order to cut himself off from mutability, he finds that he is indeed "Here, where men sit and hear each other groan" and that the bird, now having become distinct from him, belongs to an order of things totally unrelated to the world of mutability.

In the next unit of two stanzas, four and five, motivated by the proposal to reach the bourne of heaven on the wings of Poesy, the neat structural pattern is fractured, and the themes become disordered and disproportionate. The proposal for union with the nightingale comes in the first four lines; the nightingale's status is described in the next three; and the remaining lines and all of stanza five are a long lament on the darkness of the poet in contrast to the illumination in which the nightingale exists. The sense of pattern has been shattered as the poet, in a confusing darkness, turns the direction of the poem upon his own bewilderment. But this disorder is the lawless Purgatory blind that arises from the increasing separation of poet and nightingale and the consequent oscillation between the standards of heaven and earth, which are moving farther apart.

The nightingale is now in the presence of the mystery, and the darkness of that mystery is being illuminated for it. The mystery, we recall, is "of haggard seeming, but a boon indeed." It can be a terrifying darkness, like the darkness the poet felt when he sought a reason for his own laughter—the darkness of ignorance within the mystery. But the night is tender with the nightingale; the bird lives in the mystery in comfort, and the Queen-Moon, the immortal ideal, illuminates that darkness. For the poet, however, there is no light into the mystery, except for the chance heaven-sent flashes lighting up the glooms and winding mossy ways that are our paths through this world of darkness. These dark worldly paths are very different from the shadows numberless in which the nightingale has his being, and from the dark green-recessed woods into which Hermes and the nymph fled. While the nightingale finds light in the ultimate mystery, the poet's passionate strength has so weakened that he cannot even perceive the sensuous essence, or vital principle of nature. The setting (and date of composition) of the poem is mid-May, the time to which the hawthorn belongs; but the fast-fading violets belong to April and are now disappearing, and the musk-rose is mid-May's eldest child, to be born in June. To read literally the poet's complaint that he cannot see the flowers would be meaningless, for not all the flowers are there to be perceived by the external senses. Were the poet able to " see " these flowers, he would, like Pan, be penetrating to nature's central principle, its full essence, and would be overcoming the temporality of the mortal world in which the inwardness of nature becomes manifest only fragmentarily. He would be able to see the sweets with which the season-making month impregnates nature. But the husk of nature will not open quite to the core, and, being now only a weak mortal, the poet can only guess at this inwardness as he moves about in the darkness that surrounds all earthly existence.

The nightingale and the poet have now been completely divorced, one failing to do in the physical world what the other is succeeding in doing in the immortal; only a flight *to* the nightingale could possibly reunite them. Yet, there is a curious relationship between the tone with which the poet describes the nightingale and the tone with which he describes his own blindness. The tense optative force of stanzas two and three has weakened, and the splendor of the nightingale in the light of the moon and the cluster of stars is described with a degree of awe, a hushed and regal astonishment. The floral scene in stanza five is equally splendid, and also seems surrounded by a quiet wonder; but it is the converse of awe— rather, a blind bewilderment, an astonishment that confuses.

It would be pointless to search for the initial pattern in stanza six, for the pattern has been destroyed. Bird, poet, death, and earth are mingled confusedly, and the purgatorial storm is raging wildly; and yet the turmoil of the elements takes place in the most subdued of all the stanzas, the poet's passions having fallen into something very near lethargy, although his proposal is itself the greatest intensity. The darkness that began to make its appearance in stanza four has now become complete; and the shadow of death that has hovered over the entire poem, impalpably prefigured in hemlock, Lethe, the desire to fade and dissolve, the deathliness of stanza three, and the embalmed darkness, has now become the central theme. The whole first movement of the poem is attaining its climax in stanza six.

Out of the nebulous confusion the polar extremes of the poem are about to appear vividly. In seeking ease from pain, the poet, capable of thinking only in the terms of the physical world, calls upon death, which seems to his myopic vision easeful, and asks that his " quiet breath "—his now unimpassioned soul—be taken up into the air. Out of this desire arises a larger vision, a parallel but very different truth: the nightingale is also giving up its soul— its song. But in pouring out its soul into the air, just as the poet hopes to give up his " quiet breath," the nightingale is not easeful: the soul it pours out is an ecstasy-requiem, an emotionally tense, and sensorily perceptible, song of rest for the spirit, a beauty-truth. In effect, when the poet merely wishes for death, he finds again that the nightingale has greatly outdistanced him in the opposite direction, for it is eternally dying in its earthly existence; its life on earth is a continuous giving-up of its soul.

Conversely, from the point of view of earthly existence, death for the poet can mean only having ears in vain and becoming a sod. In a sense, the nightingale is the symbol of the poet's soul, and the poet is only the earthly self: death is both the heavenward flight of the soul and the material decay of mortal man's identity. Ironically, although poet and nightingale have been moving farther apart since their union in the first stanza, only in the last line of stanza six, when they have moved to their opposite poles, do they once again act directly upon each other: the sod which is the poet is present amidst the high requiem of the bird. And with further irony, one aspect of the poet's wish has now become a reality: the interpenetration of nightingale and nature in stanza one suggested the interpenetration of wine and nature, and now at last the poet is in earth and is himself earth. An interpenetration that brings ease has at last come about, but it is possible with respect to the world only if man no longer is vital. However, in the very act of myopically perceiving his outer death as merely his becoming a sod, the poet has gained a greater vision, for he now sees the bird, not merely as in the presence of beauty-truth, but as the very symbol of beauty-truth.

The first movement of the poem has reached its height by thrusting to their opposite poles the nature and the aspiration of earthly man. Keats saw as the terrible and maddening tension in man the heavenward flight of his soul while his body must be " earthward press'd." This division, which he symbolized in the " Ode on a Grecian Urn " as the altar and the town, which can never learn the reason for its desolation by soul, is here symbolized by the nightingale and the sod, which is insensible of the spirit-song.

viii

In the " Ode on a Grecian Urn," it will be recalled, the filtering
out of the component parts of heaven's bourne led the poet to
question, not the meaning of that divorce, but the meaning of the
work of art that temporarily had led him to an immortality of
passion, no matter how briefly. Keats' poetic mind is working here
in the same fashion. As each effort to attain the state of the
nightingale has brought him farther back to his sole self, so each
transformation of relationships has put the bird farther from his
reach, until finally, now that matter and spirit are at opposite poles,
he must ask the meaning of this symbolic bird, who is all that
remains to the poet of his experience, and who with apparent
incongruity sings ecstatically a song of repose for the spirit
although it does so wholly in this world of mutable things. Out
of these apparent contradictions arises the full meaning of the
nightingale. In the " Ode on a Grecian Urn," upon observing the
separation of the senses and the soul outside the realm of art,
Keats concluded that therefore art speaks to man of a realm where
the two are forever and harmoniously one. What he concludes
here is that the nightingale is an immortal bird. Now, of course,
nightingales are born and do die; and obviously Keats' statement
that the bird is immortal cannot make sense literally. It must be
immortal in another fashion. What has been impressed upon the
poet by his striving is that man is mortal with respect to earth;
he must die out of earth, and if he is immortal it is only with
respect to heaven. In the poem every effort of the poet to achieve
a perfect spiritual state brought him closer to the insensate clay
so long as he considered himself only in the context of his earthly
being. Man, then, is mortal in the sense that his earthly existence
is a movement towards a future immortality.

But the nightingale, the vision has revealed, pours out its
ecstasy-requiem while it exists on earth. It has its heaven on earth,

it experiences beauty-truth here, as man cannot. Being born *for* death, man is therefore mortal; not being born *for* death, the bird is immortal (not designed for death) with respect to the world, as man can be immortal only with respect to his postmortal existence. The full meaning of man is not completed in this world; but the nightingale, by experiencing beauty-truth here, completes its total purpose within the physical world and therefore is immortal with respect to it.

The nightingale, therefore, like the urn, remains in midst of other woe than ours, although to the poet the experience has taken place in a " passing night." The nightingale's earthly existence being its own end and therefore not designed that it might lead to a death, the symbolic bird is outside the context of time and space within which the poet has his earthly being. And this symbolic nightingale, being itself a manifestation of beauty-truth, a heaven on earth, may therefore address not only man's senses but also his spirit, and may address to his sense-spirit a song that is both ecstasy and repose, both dynamic and static: a song, that is, that partakes of the oxymoronic nature of heaven's bourne. Hence man's earthly existence is filled with a hunger for its future spiritual fulfillment, but the nightingale is experiencing here the fullness of meaning that man can experience only hereafter: no hungry generations tread it down. In a sense, the nightingale is the urn, for both embody the experience that beauty is truth and truth beauty; and in this sense both are immortal, for death is not their vital principle, as it is the vital principle of man, driving him progressively closer to a future condition when he, too, will experience forever a beauty which is truth and a truth which is beauty.

ix

With the revelation that man is mortal because his earthly existence is a compulsion towards a future life which will give him a meaning, and with the converse revelation that the nightingale fulfills its meaningfulness in the world and is therefore immortal, the ode has reached a climax beyond which the initial movement cannot rise. All the potentialities that lay in the poet's being too happy in the bird's happiness have been released when the poet becomes a sod to the high requiem of the " immortal " bird. It will be recalled that a similar condition arose in the " Ode on a Grecian Urn," which attained its climax in the third stanza; and that there the poem could progress to a meaning only by the poet's then transforming the " ethereal " scene on the frieze into a vision of a worldly sacrificial procession moving from town to altar. Only when the insight gained from the experience with a heaven's bourne of trees, pipers, and lovers was translated into the context of the mortal world in which life is a passage to a future heaven, could the full meaning of the urn be discovered.

The mode of poetic procedure in the two odes is remarkably similar, for in stanza seven of the " Ode to a Nightingale " there is a similar transmutation of the imagery as the poet searches for the meaningfulness of the experience. Up to this point the only elements of the drama have been the poet, the nightingale, and nature; but since the drama is completed at the end of stanza six by the antipodal positions to which poet and nightingale are at last driven, only by bringing his experience to bear upon a new frame of reference—the worldly frame of reference made up of emperor and clown, Ruth, and magic casements—can the poet hope to give the vision dimensions of value to man. Since the bird is not born *for* death and therefore sings a song which is of the oxymoronic nature of heaven's bourne, all men at all times—from emperor to clown— had available this knowledge of beauty-truth, this promise of a futurity when the intense passions of this world will exist without mutability and outside dimensions and selfhood. And this knowledge can be gained from the nightingale's song, which is its soul, exactly as it can be learned from the artistic vision that has been captured on the urn and that is its soul. Or, to seek a special symbol of man's inherent yearning: the Biblical Ruth, sick for home—that home ethereal, from which she is kept by only " a fragile bar "—perhaps took into her heart the ecstasy-requiem of the nightingale as she stood amid the alien corn of this world (although it is not alien to the nightingale) ; for the nightingale's song is the ecstatic repose of that home for which she yearned and from which man is temporarily exiled. Ruth is all mortals who have had the spiritual aspiration for the meaning of life and have realized that in this alien world they cannot attain the full purpose of their being. (Is there not a strong suggestion that here the Biblical name serves also as a personification of " ruth " and in this sense encompasses all mortality ?)

In the world of decay the nightingale creates this vision by living its heaven on earth, and thereby gives man a glimpse of the promise that the future holds out. It makes magic the casements ("magic" is proleptic in line 69) just as the magic union of Porphyro and Madeline opened the doors of the castle; and it opens them to the mystery, the elfin storm, for the beauty-truth song it sings is itself the mystery which permeates human life. The nightingale, like Pan, is a " firmament reflected in a sea "—a heaven on earth; and therefore, like Pan, it is the " opener of the mysterious doors / Leading to universal knowledge." It appears probable that Keats first wrote " ruthless seas " instead of " perilous seas "; and the original word more closely corresponds to the haggard-seeming of the elfin storm, which nevertheless is a boon indeed. Because the bird's song is the mystery, the perception of its meaning will open the casements into lost fairy lands, the same fairy lands of the elfin grot which are without time, space, and identity.

For the moment it appears that the poem will follow the same course as the " Ode on a Grecian Urn " after all and that the poet will pluck from his experience some conviction of a future existence for man which corresponds to the earthly " dying " of the nightingale. Keats seems to have gained insight into the nature of heaven through the " etherealizing " of the nightingale's song, to have translated that insight into the texture of human existence, and to be about to synthesize thesis and antithesis. But if he should conclude with a clear affirmation of values, he would be working contrary to the course of his materials. At best, the conflicts within the first six stanzas permit only irresolutions. Having no standard law of either heaven or earth, shifting his perspective violently from one to the other without possibility of finding a center, the poet can only guess that *perhaps* this is the meaning of the nightingale's song, for he can see only from the perspective of the " passing night " of mortal man's life, the blindness that surrounds all temporal existence before man himself can become immortal.

Because the poem cannot, therefore, reach a resolution, there must be yet another transmutation of the *données*. In stanza seven the experience of the first six stanzas had been reviewed in universal worldly terms; the translation of the " immortal " bird into the framework of the world of universal man had suggested the possibility of a meaning. But since the poem cannot arrive at a meaning, the poet once again transmutes his materials so that they appear in the texture, not of human universals, but of transiency, the world of dimensions and empty physical realities, the world in which a nightingale's song is only a song. To achieve this last metamorphosis, the poem pivots on the word " forlorn " and violently inverts itself with a terrible confusion of standards. The fairy lands are " forlorn " because they must be lost to man so long as he is in the mortal world. They are the mystery, but they cannot be peopled by mortals, for human existence involves an ignorance of the mystery even though the mystery is the central principle of man's life. But the word suddenly reverses its own value as it is torn from a context of universal man and applied to a particular man in a particular place and at a particular time. That the fairy lands are forlorn—deserted, lost—is a " good," a boon indeed; but the poet's frame of reference throughout the poem persists in being mortal, and suddenly it is the poet himself who, by contemplating the mystery, is forlorn—lost to the mortal world. To step beyond " the bourn of care, / Beyond the sweet and bitter world " is

> *O horrible! to lose the sight of well remember'd face,*
> *Of Brother's eyes, of Sister's brow.*[21]

The consequence is the poet's realization that in the mortal world to contemplate the mystery, to seek to enter into it, is to be lost to the world. And now that the poet is fully out of his vision and is once again only a creature of the mutable world, along with the transmutation of the values of " forlorn " everything in the vision reappears as its opposite, the mutable world being the inverse of the vision.

This reversal of standards is brilliantly caught up in the ambiguity of the word " toll." The recollection of his isolation from man as a result of travelling " Beyond the sweet and bitter world " summons the poet back to his own self so that he is once again self-contained, no longer participating in essence, and therefore merely a mortal. But the tolling of the bell is both a summons of his soul back to his self and also the announcement of a death. The nightingale lives its death, dying being its true living; the poet has found that, from an earthly point of view, his own death is merely to become a meaningless sod. And yet there has been a death, for only during the vision has his soul truly been " living," as the nightingale has truly been " living " by pouring forth its soul on earth. Now that his soul has returned to his self, the poet has

[21] " Lines Written in the Highlands after a Visit to Burns's Country," 29-30, 33-34.

" died " back into life. Or, to establish clearer standards, if we assume that true " life " is experiencing the condition of heaven's bourne, then the nightingale " lives " on earth but the poet cannot; and the poet's return to this world is therefore a " dying " that is announced by the same death-knell that summons him back to what most men call " life."

The first seven stanzas have taken place outside the context of time and space, but the poet's return to physical reality thaws the static scene, shakes time and space into activity: the bird now moves through space, which has until now been an irrelevant factor in the poem. And yet the irony lies in the fact that it was the poet who was striving to move to the nightingale, but that it is the nightingale who eventually moves. Consequently the enthusiastic " Away! away! " of stanza four, which announced the poet's hope for reunion with the symbol, is sadly echoed in the words " Adieu! adieu! " which recognize the futility of the aspiration, release the tension of the vision, and send the now physical bird through a spatial world. The ecstasy-requiem of the bird's song, now that it is being heard by only sensory ears, is merely the sad sweetness, the melancholy joy, that, according to the " Ode to Melancholy," characterizes the experience of beauty in the physical world—a " plaintive anthem." The poet had hoped to fade away from the mutable world into the shadows numberless in order to avoid the inherent fadingness of mortal man; but in the physical, spatial inversion of the vision it is the bird's song, the poet finds, that " fades." To the poet the night was " passing," but now the bird, who seemed fixed in darkness, passes.

And at last the final irony: the poet who had hoped for death that he might truly live—only to find that this death can have no meaning in the world—and who had discovered it is the visionary bird who has this true life even within the confines of the physical world, now discovers that in the spatial fabric of things it is the bird's song that becomes " buried " in the next valley glades. But such a series of inversions is inevitable. Because the elements of the poem are in irreconcilable conflict with each other, the poet's return to the spatial world can only turn his vision topsy-turvy and leave him with the same confusion of standards. Was it a true perception into the beauty-truth that is to come—a penetration into that immortality that man calls " death "? or was it only a fiction of the inventive faculty? " Do I wake or sleep? " The poet knows only that perhaps the same song was heard by Ruth. If it was the same, he has had a vision; if not, only a waking dream. Very early in his career Keats had asked:

> *Can death be sleep, when life is but a dream,*
> *And scenes of bliss pass as a phantom by?*
> *The transient pleasures as a vision seem,*
> *And yet we think the greatest pain's to die.*
>
> *How strange it is that man on earth should roam,*
> *And lead a life of woe, but not forsake*
> *His rugged path; nor dare he view alone*
> *His future doom which is but to awake.*[22]

X

Until now we have been examining mainly the ironic conflicts in the poem, such as the series of tauntingly irreconcilable interpretations and values of the death that begins with the burial of the wine in the " deep-delved earth " and ends with the bird's song " buried deep " in the valley glades—that begins with the poet's desire to fade from fadingness and ends with the fading of the song of the bird that a moment before was seen as immortal. And yet there is an over-all framework dominating the entire poem that, although it does not reconcile these contradictions, gives them a comprehensive relationship and imparts to them a design. The

[22] " On Death."

aspiration for fellowship with essence, Keats wrote, shadows " our own Soul's daytime / In the dark void of Night." It is noticeable that in stanzas one to three and in stanza eight there is no suggestion of darkness, and that the darkness which begins in stanza four grows thicker until the concluding stanza. In the opening stanza the poet seems able to see the green of the beech trees, and in the last stanza, after the passing of the metaphoric night, he observes the scene over which the nightingale passes. The opening and close of the poem, then, take place in the material world, the soul's daytime.

But the core of the poem is the search for the mystery, the unsuccessful quest for light within its darkness, both spatial (the forest) and temporal (the night) ; and that quest leads only to an increasing darkness, or a growing recognition of how impenetrable the mystery is to mortals. There is no light for the poet in the verdurous glooms of the world ; he cannot see into the embalmed darkness ; surrounded by darkness, he can only listen to the soul-song of the nightingale ; his quest for death is the desire for the midnight of his life, instead of his soul's daytime ; and at last he recognizes that mortal life is itself a " passing night." The " passing night " is ambivalent, for if the poet has had a true vision, he has seen momentarily into the " good " darkness, and if his is only a waking dream, it is the existence of man that is a transitory moment of dark ignorance ; but the " good " darkness, spatial and temporal, is the persistent and proper condition of the nightingale's existence. Suddenly, when the poet has returned fully into himself, the darkness is gone ; there is light, but no insight into the mystery.

On the other hand, until the last stanza the nightingale is also in darkness—among " shadows numberless " and in the " forest dim." But this is far from the agonizing darkness in which the poet gropes for standards, for this is also the darkness of the mystery—the green-recessed woods into which Hermes and the nymph fled. And yet this darkness is not cruel to the nightingale. The bird is not tormented by it as the poet is, for here there is the light of the ideal, the visionary power of penetration into the mystery. And for this reason the bird is encouraged to pass from the " shadows number-less " of the plot to the richer darkness of the " forest dim," the deeper heart of the mystery.

There are, then, two kinds of darkness and two kinds of light in the poem, just as there are two kinds of death, two kinds of fading: the poet is in the darkness of ignorance and bewilderment, the nightingale in the darkness of the mystery; light to the poet is only a return from the mystery, a withdrawal into the physical world to which his faculties are adequate, but to the nightingale light is the illumination of the mystery. Against the backdrop of these " good " and " bad " darknesses and " good " and " bad " lights, the incessant ironies and clashes within the poem take on their consistency. For example, the poet's desire to fade into the dim forest is a desire to penetrate into the mystery and hence avoid the " bad " fadingness. But this pattern of metaphysical chiaroscuro gives the poem only a consistency, not a resolution.

And the poet can end only with the unreconciled standards of a Purgatory blind. Has he glimpsed into the beauty-truth to come, or is it all a fiction? There is nothing in the experience to give him an answer. If we distort the emphasis slightly by underscoring the supposition that the experience was only a fiction, we may say that early in May, 1819, Keats had uttered his Everlasting No. In the previous month he had written " La Belle Dame Sans Merci," his Center of Indifference. But late in May, 1819, Keats was spirited strong enough to elicit from these shattering visions the Everlasting Yea of his " Ode on a Grecian Urn."

Afterword

JF I MAY, for the sake of further speculation, be allowed to assume that these readings of Keats' poems are just, they seem to imply some need for re-evaluating not only Keats but also the other major Romantics and, therefore, the position of Romanticism in the English literary tradition. The true tradition, as it is understood by many modern critics, seems to have leaped over the eighteenth and nineteenth centuries and to have settled down once again in our own day. It did not persist in a straight line because, so the interpretation runs, during those dark ages imagery was understood to be accessory, instead of functional. The criterion of the direct line of descent, Mr. Cleanth Brooks writes in his *Modern Poetry and the Tradition*, is that images be " poetic in the only sense in which objects can ever be legitimately poetic—they [must] function integrally in a poem." And the argument is that in Neo-classic and Romantic literature the normative use of imagery is ornamental ; some images were considered poetic in themselves and were laid over a poem for their power to please. Certainly there is much in the critical theory of those centuries to bear out this assumption of a hiatus during which heart and head went separate ways ; but critical theory, especially if it is read too literally, can be a dangerous guide to art as it is actually practiced.

What I should like to question is whether there has ever been a break in this " tradition," the touchstone of which I take to be the organicism of the works of art. Let me approach my point through a passage in a book that has become the graduate student's *vade mecum*. In his frequently admirable contribution to *A Literary History of England* Professor Samuel Chew has written that the " Ode to a Nightingale " is " almost perfect," but " the description of the nightingale's song as a ' plaintive anthem ' in the final stanza contradicts, and jars ever so slightly upon, the earlier indications of its happiness and ecstasy. What had been purely objective becomes subjective." As I understand the poem, this description is accurate in every detail. But the frame of reference is quite wrong. From the position Mr. Chew has chosen, the governing pattern of the poem involves the happiness and ecstasy of the bird and an objectivity of presentation. Anything that contradicts this pattern is a flaw, for then the contradictions are not functioning at all or are not functioning integrally. The account of what is going on in the last stanza of the ode is perceptive, but the assumption behind Mr. Chew's evaluation is that he has access to the true scheme of things and that the poet failed to fulfill that scheme. In other words, there seems to be something left over in the poem because this residue cannot be crammed into the critic's assumptions. If this residue is disturbing, we call it a contradiction or the poet's lapse; if in itself it is not unpleasant, we call it ornament. It would be more gracious if we were to ask whether the hypothesis we have brought to the poem is sufficiently embracing.

To say, then, that the imagery is inconsistent with the poem or that it is a superfluous layer of decoration may mean nothing more than that one does not fully recognize the order of things within which it is functional. Something of this sort, I judge, is going on when Mr. Allen Tate writes of the " Ode on a Grecian Urn " that " the entire last stanza, except the phrase ' Cold Pastoral ' (which probably ought to be somewhere else in the poem) is an illicit commentary added by the poet to a ' meaning ' which was symbolically complete at the end of the preceding stanza, number four." Certainly it is what is taking place when he says that, having extracted the nightingale symbol, Keats does not know what to do with the physical nightingale " except to make it, in the last stanza, fly away "; and when he says that the assertion of the bird's immortality is " out of form in an obvious sense, for the poem is an accumulation of pictorial situations, and the claim of immortality for the bird is dramatic and lyrical."

If, as I believe, there is no such thing as a " tradition," but only the repeated creation of works of art, then the history of literature is not one of appearances and disappearances of organicism, but one of changing artistic designs and patterns of thought in terms of which the corresponding art is organic in varying degrees. For example, Mr. Brooks has contrasted the supposedly afunctional, ornamental imagery of the Romantics with the compass image in Donne's " Valediction: Forbidding Mourning " to show that the compass image is poetic because it functions integrally in the poem. It is not functional to me, however, if it is essential to my system of things that the circle drawn by a compass is only a crude, highly imperfect imitation of the ideal circle; or, again, if in my system of thought the straight line is the shape of perfection. It is only when I enter Donne's universe and agree to believe that the circle is the nature of God, the world, man's head—is the necessary form of perfection—that the image is able to function integrally in the poem. Otherwise, it must jar, even " ever so slightly." It would be wrong, therefore, to say that the compass is not " poetic " in itself; it is poetic in the only sense in which objects can ever be legitimately poetic—it inheres in a particular ordering of things and values and therefore has the power of working organically in a poem controlled by that order.

Or let us take another element that has governed the monistic idea of a " tradition " in English literature that coyly comes and goes. The irony that has so frequently been found to be the core of organic interrelationships contributes to organicism only if an ironic view is relevant to the frame of the particular work of art. Irony is not integration, but a particular way to integrate; it is not an end, but a special means—unless, of course, we now extend further the already strained meaning of the word to embrace every mode of fusing disparate elements. There is irony in the " Ode on a Grecian

Urn " in the opposition of the love that is " forever warm " and the
" Cold Pastoral," and in the " Ode to a Nightingale " in the Janus-
like value of " forlorn " and in the multivalences of death, dark,
light. But this irony is not merely a literary device Keats has
chosen for securing organicism because he knows the secret of art;
it derives necessarily from the peculiar metaphysics within which
he writes, for that pattern of thought requires that he strive to
reconcile the mortal with the immortal without canceling either.

Irony, then, is only that mode of expression which, by departing
in opposite directions at the same time, provides for the artistic
integration of contrarieties, not for the artistic fusion of all kinds of
disparate materials. Wordsworth's frame of thought, on the other
hand, does not usually involve oppositions, and consequently it is
unprofitable to search in such a poem as the " Solitary Reaper " for
wit, paradox, ambiguity, irony, and tension. Its mode of organicism
is proportionately as different from these modes as its metaphysics
is different from the ones they belong to.

Why, then, has the modern reader been less successful in perceiving the integrity of eighteenth- and nineteenth-century art than
he has that of the earlier art? The answer is really the same as the
one to the question: why did those two centuries fail to recognize
the integrity of seventeenth-century metaphysical poetry? The
structure of our own culture has given us a pattern of thought
closer to that of the seventeenth century than to that of any other
age. The two are sufficiently akin so that we tend without special
effort to bring to metaphysical poetry much of the pattern in which
its elements are functional; but for the same reason the materials
of Romantic art have refused to work for us without special assistance. The phenomenon is not peculiar to us. When the eighteenth
century had lost sight of the Renaissance cosmology in which elements of the physical, of the moral, and of the spiritual orders of
things were analogically related to each other, it came to be felt

that metaphysical use of imagery was extravagant, not in accord with reality. In Dr. Johnson's phrase, metaphysical poems were "heterogeneous ideas yoked with violence together." Something was left over that jarred; not everything fitted into Johnson's pattern.

It is now comparatively easy to reconstruct the designs of thought and the patterns of artistic arrangement before the nineteenth century because those orderings were then rather widely held and understood: the controls might be, either singly or in combination, the literary kinds, classical mythology, a universe of analogous planes, Christianity, courtly love, Platonism, the Great Chain of Being, etc. The individual variations within these systems were slight enough so that we may usually allow the given work of art to mark out its own modifications. But in reading the literature of the nineteenth century and thereafter the problem is considerably more difficult. For with the nineteenth century almost all accredited systems of ordering experience had broken down. Each artist has had to make his poetic world before he could make his poems, because he first has had to work out the functional relations of his experiences. Wordsworth worked out his pattern; Shelley his; Keats his. I suspect that our failure to grasp as total and integrated experiences such works as Shelley's "Adonais" or Emily Brontë's *Wuthering Heights* or E. M. Forster's *A Passage to India* results from our not having succeeded as yet in bringing to these works the proper controlling cosmos, for each cosmos is the creation of the author. Instead of describing our personal responses or lamenting that Wordsworth is not Donne, we need to re-examine the Romantics and their successors in order to discover whether within each one's frame of things he created, not *Romantic* art or *Victorian* art—not works inside or outside a "tradition"—but art. Something of this sort I have tried to do in these chapters for Keats.